THE DOCTOR RODE SIDE-SADDLE

THE DOCTOR RODE SIDE-SADDLE

Ruth Matheson Buck

McClelland and Stewart Limited

ISBN 0-7710-1735-9

McClelland and Stewart Limited
The Canadian Publishers
25 Hollinger Road, Toronto

to the memory of John Grace
and our mother the doctor

Foreword

This is the story of a woman who practised Medicine in the Territory of the Saskatchewan from 1898 to 1918.

Elizabeth Matheson was born in 1866, and lived with spirit to the age of ninety-two; yet she counted as the fulfilment of her life "the years with Grace", from 1891 to 1916, when she was the wife of John Matheson.

He was born in 1848 in Kildonan on the Red River, where there were many other John Mathesons. There was only one "John Grace", and he carried the nickname with lively zest, far beyond Kildonan, into the Territory of the Saskatchewan.

Of the children born to John and Elizabeth Matheson, I was the seventh; and only ten years old when my father died. Yet twenty years later, when I began to gather notes on the early years of his colourful life, I found the key that could instantly unlock delighted memory. It was the simple statement: "I'm a daughter of John Grace."

My interest in the story of Lord Selkirk's settlers at Red River, and the history of early years in the Territory of the Saskatchewan, had been quickened in 1931 by Campbell Innes of Battleford, and by my aunt, Eleanor Shepphird Matheson, who gave me my uncle's collection of papers and his library of western history.

My first resolve was to write the story of my mother's life, and it was she who insisted, "It's not my story but your father's that you should be writing." That was not possible, though I was led to make as careful a study as I could of his family and boyhood in Kildonan Settlement, and of his early years in the Territory of the Saskatchewan.

Only indirect references appear in this account, yet those experiences of his youth were the foundation to all John Matheson's later work and his was the force that directed and gave full meaning to my mother's achievements. Moreover, the search was essential to my own understanding of a father whom I remembered only as an old man, when his strength had failed and his life was ending.

I began by gathering notes from many who remembered John Grace in his youth, including his sisters, Christiana Cunningham (1850-1937) of Battleford, and Elizabeth Lamb (1859-1949) of Winnipeg; and his cousin, the Most Reverend Samuel Pritchard Matheson (1852-1942), formerly Archbishop of Rupert's Land and Primate of All Canada, who had retired and was writing his own reminiscences of the Settlement at Red River. I must acknowledge as well my indebtedness to two of the next generation of Lord Selkirk's settlers, Elisabeth Henderson of St. James, and her sister, Anne Matheson Henderson, historian of the Lord Selkirk Association of Rupert's Land.

I have been particularly fortunate throughout in the patient collaboration of my eldest sister, Gladys Crim, and in the encouragement of all our family.

The most remarkable assistance came from Elizabeth Matheson herself. Not the least incident in this story has needed invention, and practically every one is drawn from her personal recollections, in notes that I gathered until 1956. She was ninety then, and when she read the completed typescript that I sent to her, she wrote: "I cannot thank you sufficiently for the love that has inspired, strengthened and aided you throughout this long self-imposed task. . . . You have drawn a picture of a much finer woman than I presented to those about me but perhaps they saw more than I realized and were lenient in their judgment. It has brought back happy days to me and I read it with the feeling of having known the woman you were writing about."

It is years since I first resolved that I would write her story, and it is difficult to trace exact sources of material that I have shaped and re-shaped; or to acknowledge all the help that I received. There have been many who have encouraged me, and whom I remember with gratitude though their names may not appear in these notes. Still, the work might never have been revised and brought to a satisfactory completion had it not been for the interest of Dr. Henrietta Banting of Toronto, whose encouragement prompted me to this further effort.

Over the years, I have consistently checked each reminiscence against my own reading in the history of Red River and the Territory of the Saskatchewan; in early reports of that Diocese; and in accounts of the first women to enter the field of Medicine in Canada.

On four occasions, I have had assistance from members of the staff at the Public Archives of Canada, but my chief indebtedness in that area is to Saskatchewan Archives, both in Regina and Saskatoon. I would express my thanks particularly to Dr. Lewis H. Thomas, now of the University of Alberta; to Allan R. Turner, Provincial Archivist; and to Dr. John H. Archer, who as Principal of Regina Campus, University of Saskatchewan, still found time in 1972 to read a revision of the manuscript.

A full list of books, periodicals, and published or unpublished articles that I have read, may seem out of proportion to the part they played, beyond providing the background for my work in assembling Elizabeth Matheson's own story.

It is a remarkable one, and she told it with revealing honesty. Her garment ever was simplicity, which her children have come to name courage and nobility.

Ruth Matheson Buck

One

Elizabeth Scott's first meeting with John Matheson at the Cook's Creek picnic in August of 1885 might have had no real significance for her, and so have passed from her memory, had it not been for the constancy of his love for her from that day on.

He was thirty-seven, and would write to her later: "My love for you never has changed and never can, whatever may come between us. The love of a man my age is altogether different from the passion of a boy of twenty. . . ." She was only nineteen, and the greater difference than age between them lay in the courses of their lives—his in the reckless freedom of the plains of the Saskatchewan and the mountains of British Columbia, hers in the narrow restraint of farming communities in Ontario and Manitoba. It would be six years before she agreed to marry him—years that for her would be given to high endeavour and far travel, crowding from her mind any consideration of marriage to John Matheson.

It was her brother instead who set the goal she strove to attain. Thomas Scott had recognized his young sister's ability and had made it possible for her to leave the farm at Morris to attend high school in Winnipeg and obtain her teaching certificate. Tom was completing a final year of teaching in Manitoba before entering Queen's University; and he secured a position for Elizabeth in the school district of Sunnyside, adjoining his own at Cook's Creek. On her part, there was only the faint hope that she might follow him to Kingston, where others like herself had ventured into the field of higher education, and where the Women's Medical College had been established.

When Elizabeth had taught for only a week at Sunnyside, she was invited to Neil Henderson's home, where Tom was boarding. It was her first meeting with the Henderson family, but she was drawn at once into their friendship, scarcely thinking of them as strangers. Jim Scott, her oldest brother, had been coming from Morris at every opportunity to court Jennie, Neil Henderson's daughter by a previous marriage; and Tom's attention centered upon Jennie's half-sister, Nellie.

Mrs. Henderson was a daughter of Lord Selkirk's settlers at Kildonan, and John Matheson's favourite aunt. He visited her home whenever he returned to Red River, and on this occasion had promised to join the family before they left for the picnic where the whole community would gather.

Their references to "John Grace" or simply "Grace" intrigued

Elizabeth. Nicknames in a Scottish community were common, but usually revealing, and she asked how this one had been given. "It was that lively way of his, even as a child," his aunt told her. "Never quiet, always some excitement, some adventure to tell. When the family sat down to a meal, it was just the same. His father would have to rap the table hard, and call: 'John—Grace'. The other children caught it up, and then the whole Settlement. It marked him from all the other John Mathesons—seemed just the right name for him. No one can forget John Grace. There's not another like him."

In the morning, while Mrs. Henderson and the girls finished their last preparations, Elizabeth waited on the steps outside the door, looking across the yard to where young Angus Henderson and Tom were hitching the horses to a wagon. She did not hear the quiet tread of moccasins approaching by the side path, and John Matheson's voice surprised her.

"You must be Miss Scott."

He had lifted a somewhat battered Western hat to introduce himself, and sunlight glinted on the crisp auburn-red hair and clipped beard of a tall handsome man in the full vigour of strength. He stood on the pathway just below her, his eyes on a level with her own, and most deeply blue, alert with interest; but his voice had brought a burst of greetings from both house and yard, a sudden flurry of movement in which Elizabeth took only a quiet part.

As the wagon moved from the house, she found herself seated at the back with the girls and their mother, picnic boxes between them and the four men, who stood at the front, balancing easily as the horses broke into a quick trot. She listened only casually to the light chatter of the girls, her ear tuned to the deeper undertones of the men's voices, as they spoke of horses and farms, of railroad building and politics.

It was when the Saskatchewan Rebellion was mentioned that Tom fell silent, and she remembered his advice. "Keep away from all that, Lizzie. These people don't look on that uprising as we from Ontario do. Remember they've been here through generations now, these descendants of fur-traders and of Lord Selkirk's settlers. It's only fifteen years since this whole territory became part of Canada; and to them, those of us who have come lately from the east are still 'Canadians'—newcomers at best—sometimes interlopers, wanting everything our own way, and more than a little responsible for the uprisings under Louis Riel, here in '70, and again this year on the Saskatchewan. They had lived at peace for more than fifty years with the Indians and half-breeds, and many of them—I think John Matheson's as good an example as any—are really more in sympathy with the rebels and

10

what they call their 'grievances' than with the Government forces that suppressed the rebellions. Some of our eastern papers have spoken harshly of 'white rebels' who may or may not have taken any actual part in the fighting, but are accused now of 'treason-felony', a few of them directly charged and facing trial."

That there could be any sympathy for rebellious Indians and half-breeds seemed incredible to Elizabeth, recalling the fears and excitement of the spring, when their own brave volunteers had left Winnipeg for the Saskatchewan conflict. She had been tearful then herself at parting with one young man, though now that he was safely returned she wanted only to end the understanding that she was willing to marry him.

As she listened to the men, she realized that there was an indication of that sympathy in John Matheson's comments, but he had turned the conversation with what seemed only a light remark about needing a gun. Neil Henderson's sharp question silenced even the girls. "What do you want with another? You were proud enough a year ago of that fine new Winchester you had."

Matheson turned to look directly at his uncle, and his face, now in Elizabeth's full view, was entirely serious. "I lent it," he said, with slow deliberation, "last January. Before I left the Territories for British Columbia. To Gabriel Dumont. We were friends, and he asked for it. To hunt moose. If it wasn't lost at Batoche, then it's over the border with him, in Montana. I don't expect to see it again."

Then Tom was right. John Matheson was one at heart with the rebels, even with the fiery commander of Riel's forces. Elizabeth drew her breath sharply. Quite unexpectedly, his eyes met hers, wide with amazement, and she felt a surge of warm colour flood her face.

The silence held for a moment; then there was a sudden whir of wings, a bird fluttering from the road ahead of the horses. It was young, still uncertain of its wings, wavering in its flight.

"Wait a bit," Matheson called to the driver, and leaped from the wagon. The bird had fallen near the road. He caught it readily, and sprang lightly to the back of the wagon, to stand near Elizabeth. "A gift for teacher," he said with smiling gentleness, and laid it in her hands.

Nellie's voice came with soft emphasis. "That's John Grace for you. He *charms* birds." Elizabeth's tension was released in amusement. She lifted mocking hazel-green eyes, to meet again the intensity that sought response she would not give.

The frightened heart of the bird beat against her hands. She said, with dry implication, "Then here is one that can't easily be charmed," and leaning past John Grace, extended her arms beyond the wagon before she opened her hands, gently and slowly, to release the captive. Surprisingly, the bird was calm now, and stayed quietly on her palms, seeming aware of its freedom and waiting only until it was ready to test its wings once more in flight.

For Elizabeth, the rest of the day would pass with equal assurance. She knew that the picnic had been planned as the district's farewell to her brother; and when they joined the gathering, she listened with warm pride to the people's expressions of regret that he was leaving them, fully aware of the respect and friendship they felt for him, and which they were willing to extend to his sister.

John Grace, too, was surrounded by friends, but in the late afternoon he came to find Elizabeth. "Your brother tells me that you want to go back to your boarding-house at Oakbank. If you'll let me, I'd like to drive you. Jack Skuce has a fine black horse and rig that he'll lend me."

She accepted willingly; and on the five-mile drive listened with interest to his entertaining stories of early years in the territory of the Saskatchewan. He was returning to British Columbia, and she would not see him again, but when his first letter came, she was not surprised. She wrote a friendly answer, and other letters followed, some at long intervals, and with strange postmarks as he went from one contract to another wherever railroad construction continued. He addressed her as Miss Scott, yet the formal salutation could never quite restrain his lively comments; and she seemed to hear him speak, to feel again the suppressed excitement of his disturbing presence.

She was enjoying her work, was happier in teaching at Sunnyside than during her previous short terms in other districts farther up the Red River. She missed her brother's companionship, but her friendship with the Hendersons strengthened. They referred often to John Grace, and she was quite aware that, with the rest of the community, they knew of the letters that came to her, and surmised much more from the interest he had shown in her.

She learned something of his boyhood in Kildonan and of his adventurous youth on the plains; and more details were added when she went the next year, at a higher salary, to teach the school at Poplar Point, west of Winnipeg. Matheson's sister, Christiana Cunningham, lived there and her children attended the school.

Elizabeth often went to their farm—invited, she was certain, at John Grace's special request, for Christiana's talk centered about him and their Kildonan home, skirting his reckless years in the Territories, preferring rather to speak about their younger brother Edward Matheson's entirely

12

Elizabeth Scott, Manitoba school-teacher (1885).

different course in that same vast area, where he had become an ordained clergyman of the Anglican Church.

She told of Edward's service as teacher on the Indian Reserves of Mistawasis and Ahtahkakoop; of his studies in theology when Emmanuel College was opened in Prince Albert; of his faithfulness to the people in his charge at St. Catherine's in that troubled area, all through the Rebellion; of his steadfast witness on their behalf in the trials that followed.

When she turned again to John Grace, Christiana would dwell upon his ability as trader, freighter and guide across the plains; his success in the new railroad work, the bridges he had built across the Fraser River, the contracts he readily obtained. "There's nothing that my brother can't turn his hand to," she would assert. "He earns a good living—should settle down. It's time he married."

Elizabeth learned to switch the subject adroitly to the progress of the Cunningham children in school, or back to Christiana's own childhood in Kildonan with her brothers and sisters.

Two

John Grace had been the first of seven children born to Hugh Matheson and his wife Letitia, a daughter of John Pritchard—"our English grandfather", Christiana would stress, as though in apology, for Hugh Matheson's parents had come from Sutherlandshire with the party of 1815. Pritchard was from Shrewsbury, and he had come in 1801 to be a fur-trader, first with the XY and then with the North-West Company, before he joined the Colony at Red River, and married a young widow from Nairn, who had come with the first party of settlers in 1812.

He had been a well-educated man, a leader in the Colony, Lord Selkirk's secretary, agent for the Selkirk estate, and member of the first Council of Assiniboia. In comparison to the other settlers, he was a man of substance, and he built a large house on the east bank of the river, "The Elms", which was also a boarding-school for the sons of Hudson's Bay Company officers in distant posts.

Though Pritchard was supposedly a business man, it was in the establishment of churches and schools for the Settlement that his primary interest lay—while the failure of one business venture after another cost the Selkirk estate large sums of money, and took most of Pritchard's as well.

Yet it was his generosity in times of great adversity, the wages that he paid, the whole-hearted support he gave the settlers to make their lives

Two of the original settlers at Red River: John Matheson's grandparents, Angus and Christiana Matheson (*c*. 1870).

endurable, that redeemed the Englishman at last in their eyes; for there had been one great transgression in 1820 that had seemed to them unforgivable. At that time Pritchard had returned from England, after the Earl's untimely death, not with the Presbyterian minister promised to the settlers from the Highlands, but with an Anglican clergyman, the Reverend John West, the first Protestant missionary in all Rupert's Land. They held Pritchard directly responsible for that broken promise.

The Roman Catholic mission of St. Boniface had been established in 1818. Not until 1851, did the Presbyterians have their own Kildonan Church, under the Reverend John Black, who came from Upper Canada, and spoke no Gaelic. During all those years, the Scottish settlers had had to accept the Anglican ministry—and some of the clergy they came to revere; but in 1851, three hundred of them left the Anglican Church, taking with them many of Pritchard's grandchildren.

Two of his daughters had married staunchly Presbyterian Mathesons, the elder dying with the birth of her eighth child, a son, in 1852. Hugh Matheson's wife nursed her sister's child with her own baby girl, until he was strong enough to be given into the care of his grandfather's household at "The Elms". This was Samuel Pritchard Matheson, destined for the highest office of the Anglican Church in Canada.

John Grace was four years older than his cousin, and he attended the Kildonan school, across the river from his father's farm, until their uncle, the Reverend Samuel Pritchard, in the tradition established by John Pritchard, opened a boarding-school for boys, at Middlechurch (St. Paul's).

John Grace was a day-pupil, walking four miles from his father's farm; his cousin was living at Middlechurch, where the Pritchards had moved after

15

their father's death and the sale of "The Elms". In 1865, Samuel Matheson was one of the boys who went with their schoolmaster to establish St. John's College, eight miles up the river (the Upper Church); and it was in that College that his achievements both as scholar and athlete drew the attention of Bishop Machray, and his further education was assured.

For John Grace, all formal education had ended. His father died in 1864, of an accident three years earlier that had injured the bone of his arm. Hugh Matheson had been an able and resourceful man; and even in his suffering the work of the farm continued, with the help of his wife and children, while he taught one of the day-schools that equally hard-working settlers' children attended for only half of each week-day, to learn "reading, writing and summing".

During the last months of his life, even this was impossible for Hugh Matheson, and John Grace undertook to teach the school in addition to a major part of the farm work. He was only fifteen, but he was strong and capable; and the whole Settlement noted how earnestly he accepted the heavy responsibility when his father died.

That same year, another disaster struck when the York boats brought typhus fever from the ships at Hudson Bay. It raged through all the Settlement, and two of Hugh Matheson's children died. John Grace recovered, but his hearing was affected. When Christiana spoke of these misfortunes, and of floods, and grasshopper plagues, it seemed as though the children of that third generation, hearing their grandparents tell of the struggle simply to survive during the earlier years of conflict and bloodshed, had come to accept hardship as normal.

"We were not rich," Christiana explained needlessly, and yet with simple pride. "No one in the Settlement was. But the farm supplied our needs, and there was no debt. We had seven cows, five oxen, ten or twelve sheep, and pigs and chickens."

In the late fall of 1868, when she was eighteen and John Grace twenty, he was teaching the parish school in St. John's, and they had to work early and late. She remembered that he "limed the byre" after dark, and while she held the lantern for him they talked of all their plans. Their father had "taken out" lumber and shingles from the mill for a new house that they could build at last, for with the settlement of John Pritchard's estate their mother had inherited her portion; and they had even dared to send an order out with the York boats for John Grace's first tailor-made suit and soft dress material for the two older girls.

Christiana's voice grew bitter then. "We didn't know that our mother had decided to marry again. She told us when we finished our work that Saturday night, and the wedding was on Monday.''

The man she married was a successful farmer at Headingly, on the Assiniboine, with a fair-sized family of his own, whose wife had recently died in childbirth. It was a marriage of convenience for him; but Christiana never tried to understand why her mother had agreed. She only knew that it had shattered all their lives, in particular her own, for two years later she married her step-father's son, in spite of her mother's pleadings. She had lost all confidence in that guidance, though her wilfulness brought no happiness either, only harder work and constant pregnancies.

Everything the mother had owned became quite legally James Cunningham's when she married him. The Kildonan farm was sold, and when the York boats came the next year, the goods his step-children had ordered were sold too. The family moved to the farm at Headingly—but without John Grace. "I was kicked out," he declared.

Neil Henderson was farming at the time on the Assiniboine, only a mile or two west of Fort Garry and the small village of Winnipeg. His wife welcomed her brother's son into their home, and John Grace was engaged as teacher in their school in the parish of St. James, where the new incumbent was the Reverend William Cyprian Pinkham, soon to be appointed Manitoba's first superintendent of education for the Protestant schools, and later Bishop of Calgary and Saskatchewan.

John Grace had little heart for teaching. He had carried responsibilities too heavy for a boy, with assurance and ability far beyond his years; and everything had been suddenly wrested from him. He had lost his home and all that he had worked for; and he was disillusioned and restless, without aim or purpose.

With springtime, trains of Red River carts began their slow progress westward along the Portage trail, loaded with trading goods for distant posts in the territory of the Saskatchewan; and as summer advanced, brigades from the west appeared—buffalo-hunters with pemmican and hides, freighters for the Company, or free-traders with the season's furs. The carts passed by the hundreds along the many-rutted trail, tortured screech of wooden wheels on heavy ungreased wooden axles rending the silence of the plains.

Their camps were a magnet to every man and boy, releasing John Grace from the tedium of school and farm. In one camp he met his step-father's brother, John Cunningham, a free-trader from Lac Ste. Anne, west of Fort Edmonton; and he drew Cunningham's instant attention. School-teacher! A

17

strong young man, with no ties to hold him—and the plains stretching out there a thousand miles and more! Come with the brigade back to Lac Ste. Anne—learn to be a freighter, a trader, a buffalo-hunter.

Buffalo-hunter! What boy in the Settlement had not dreamed of that—had not watched with envious eyes the skilful horsemanship of Indian and Metis riders, racing about their encampments, man and pony melded into one, in a savage exaltation of swerving grace and speed.

Through all that troubled year, John Grace's delight had been his own swift pony, at last acquired. He would have to sell her now, buy instead a stout ox and cart. For there was no uncertainty in his mind; and when the long brigade moved "out to the Saskatchewan", he was one of the procession of drivers walking beside their lumbering carts. But there were horses and riders too, eager for the chase as soon as they reached the buffalo country—and ready to let the keen red-headed boy practise the skill.

Three months or more, the brigade would follow its course, west, northwest, ten miles a good day's average—oxen and carts mired when sloughs and mudholes were unavoidable—steep banks to negotiate at streams and rivers that they forded when they could, more often stopping for full days to unload and then reload the carts, lashing the heavy wooden wheels below to make crude rafts, and swimming the animals—patient, straining oxen, or stubborn, resisting ones—balking or responsive horses—sweating, shouting men. But there was laughter too, and in camp the scraping of fiddles, the wild release of high spirits in step-dance and jig, the songs of early voyageurs, the ballads of the plains.

Their voices were in Cree and French. To Matheson, neither was strange; and even in the first weeks of that westward journey, both came to him with easy fluency, tuned as his ear had been from boyhood at Red River, though in Kildonan the "twa tongues" still meant Gaelic and English.

The first reflected all the longing of exiles, and their strong determination to hold to the faith of their fathers, in family prayers and Bible readings —even while their English speech was trained by the liturgy of the Anglican Church, and the schooling of those clergy. Its precision amazed newcomers, unaware of the standards set by Anglican scholars, and by the officers of the Hudson's Bay Company, who were usually educated gentlemen.

Within the Pritchard connection, it was their grandfather's own influence largely, for he had been educated in the famous Shrewsbury School, one in several generations of burgesses' sons. John Grace remembered him only as an old man, in his armchair at "The Elms", beside him a year's issue of the London *Times*, brought by York boat from Hudson Bay, arranged in careful

18

order that no one dared to disturb, the pile on one side growing as the other diminished.

The children might speak to their grandmother in her native Gaelic; but when their speech was English, Pritchard would correct each slight mistake. Well beyond the swish of his grandfather's cane, John Grace had delighted to tease with "Red River bungay"—that slurred, wholly ungrammatical, amusingly expressive speech, which owed its vague derivation to English, but was rich with the cadence of both Gaelic and Cree.

Matheson had left all that behind him now—all the quiet, sober, God-fearing life of Kildonan. The bonds of kinship would never loosen, and he would come at fairly regular intervals to Red River, where Fort Garry was the distributing centre for all the North-West. But the territory of the Saskatchewan had claimed him for its own.

It was a life to which he was admirably suited, not only through his strength and quick ability, but in the qualities that won him friendship everywhere—particularly his gift for mimicry and story-telling. Every day could hold adventure for him, which he would weave into lively accounts of the last great buffalo-hunts, of mail-carrying by dog-sled and snowshoe in the first years of government service in the Territories, of freighting along the old Fort Carlton trail, of life in trading-posts and Indian encampments.

And there were other stories that drifted back to his people in Kildonan —of shrewd horse-trading, of poker-playing, even of whisky-smuggling.

"He's not bad," Christiana would insist. "Just wild. Wherever he goes there's uproar. That fiddle of his. Never without it. And the light quick step of him in the Red River jigs."

Then again—"He makes a good living though. Not a piece of work he isn't ready to tackle. It's time he married and settled down."

Three

The stories were entertaining enough, even as Christiana recounted them; and John Grace's letters from the mountains conveyed the same spirit. Elizabeth, however, was under no illusion as to life in those railroad construction camps and in the rough towns along the line. She had witnessed some of it during her school days in Winnipeg, where saloons were common, and drunken roistering men reeled along every muddy street.

In her quiet boarding-house at Poplar Point, she read the letters as they came, and answered them with news of his family and friends; but it was to her brother's letters that she responded with more feeling, convinced that it was in the life to which he was committed that any real purpose lay.

Thomas Scott would not return to Manitoba. Beginning his second year at Queen's, he wrote to her of his studies, and of his summer at Belleville, supervising the placement on farms of boys and girls from the slums of Glasgow and Manchester.

It was work financed by Miss Ellen Bilbrough, an English gentlewoman, who had built Marchmont Home in Belleville to receive these hapless children and train them for work in Canada. The Scotts had learned of the endeavour in 1875, soon after its establishment; and their father had been moved to make his own contribution from the produce of their farm at Burnbrae, and then drive throughout the community, filling his wagon with the donations of others before he went on to Belleville, another thirty miles or more.

Tom had accompanied him. At Marchmont Home, Miss Bilbrough received the unexpected gift with gratitude; and then, questioning the bright fourteen-year-old boy, learned that his education had ended in their rural school, without any real prospect of continuing farther. She offered to keep him at Marchmont Home, to attend the collegiate and to give in return what help he could in training boys who had not the least concept of farm work. Tom passed his matriculation examinations successfully, and secured his teaching certificate before he followed the family to Manitoba.

They had gone in 1878, one family in the flood of settlers seeking new land in Manitoba, even ahead of the promised railway. They had had to travel by the American line, and then down the Red River by steamboat, to arrive on the muddy bank at Fort Garry on Easter Sunday, April 23, in a wet fall of snow.

The family stayed for a few months in the fast-growing village of Winnipeg, just beyond the gates of the Hudson's Bay Company fort; but their father and their oldest brother, Jim, went back with a team of plodding oxen, forty miles up the course of the twisting river, to Morris. Jim was nineteen, and they had been able to claim a full section of land that was much richer than the hundred stoney acres at Burnbrae.

Elizabeth had been born on that farm near Campbellford, in 1866, in the large house that her grandfather had built, after he cleared the land from the forests of Northumberland County and for twenty years plied his trade as stonemason all through the area. She did not remember the rugged man, nor his gentle wife, who had run away with him to Gretna Green from her father's estate near Paisley; but the child had often been lifted to trace with

Daughters of James and Elizabeth Scott (Campbellford, Ont., 1874). Elizabeth Scott is the child on the right.

her fingers words boldly cut into an outer stone near one of the windows of the house at Burnbrae: "Jas. Scott emigrated from Scotland 1834."

At the age of four, Elizabeth attended Burnbrae school; at twelve, she was the brightest and most advanced pupil in the school at Morris; but the teacher who recognized this was accused of favouring the girl, and was summarily dismissed. The one who followed gave his attention, much more wisely for his own sake, to the chairman's son, and ignored Elizabeth entirely. Angered finally by his indifference, she hotly refused to continue, and apprenticed herself instead to the village dressmaker.

She might have remained quite satisfied with her decision, for the skill appealed to her, and she made good progress. Tom, however, in his own school at Cook's Creek, learned of the incident, and though he understood his young sister's rebellion he urged her to return to school, and arranged for her to take her matriculation in Winnipeg. At seventeen, she was a teacher.

And these few years later, Tom asked her to leave school-teaching and come to Belleville to help Miss Bilbrough. Their oldest sister Janet was at Marchmont Home as house-keeper, instructing girls in those duties; and Janet had decided that she would marry Alex MacKay and go with him to British Columbia. No one could dissuade her. Tom suggested that Elizabeth might be a replacement at Marchmont Home.

21

He had opposed her attempt to be a dressmaker, yet could overlook the fact that to continue her school studies she had left home at fourteen, and that in any case it had always been the older girls who were their mother's willing and most able assistants in the work of the household. He was quite confident that Elizabeth was as capable as skilful Janet; and because of his expectations, she set herself at once to learn all she could in the house where she boarded.

Miss Bilbrough's definite request came within a week. More than a hundred girls and boys would arrive at Belleville in March, to receive a brief training before they found places on farms. It was an urgent appeal that the school board at Poplar Point readily accepted, releasing Elizabeth from her contract with less than a month's notice.

She went first to Morris to see her parents, taking the train from Winnipeg. In 1883, she had travelled along that line to her first school, near Manitou. The roadway had not yet been ballasted, and the view from her dusty seat in the rocking, reeling coach had been alternately sky and then bare earth. The frightening ride made her violently sick, and she had climbed shakily to the station platform at Manitou, white and trembling.

The track was firm now, and she could concentrate upon the resolve she had made. In her handbag, she carried a letter that she had written to the persistent young man whom she had met while teaching at Osborne, and

Elizabeth's father, James Scott (Winnipeg, *c*. 1880).

who was still determined that she would marry him. The letter would put an end to all that, quite definitely; and she had intended to give it to his brother, the station-master.

As the train neared Osborne, she realized that even that could be an awkward meeting, and decided that she would simply toss the letter to him as the train left the station. But the light paper might be swept away by the wind of the train's passing, and would have to be weighted. She searched her bag, came upon her small pen-knife, and thrust it hurriedly though a corner of the envelope as the train drew into the station. She waited near the steps of the last coach, out of the station-master's view until the train moved on again, and then, clinging by one hand to the rail, she tossed the letter to the feet of the startled man, gave him only a quick wave of her free hand, pulled herself up the steps, and went back to her seat.

That was finished. She felt regret only for the loss of the knife. Her father had given it to her. She remembered how he had opened the small blade, and then balanced the knife on its back. "Whenever you see a knife balanced so, think of your father, lassie." She would replace the lost knife in Morris, have him hold it again in his work-hardened hands; but there would need to be no words between them. She would never forget her kindly father.

To John Matheson, she had written a happy letter expecting him to share in the adventure of her new undertaking. His answer came to her at Marchmont Home, and it conveyed a sense of troubled urgency. At Sunnyside and Poplar Point, she had been with his people, and he knew that they had kept him present in her mind. There had always been the expectation too that he could make the long journey to Red River and would meet her again. Now suddenly she was removed from everything that recalled him, everything familiar to him. Her reply was a friendly one of reassurance, yet it was true that already he seemed remote, quite of another world.

Her new work held all her attention, all her interest. Her youthful liveliness won its response from the pathetic, half-frightened girls in her charge; their need lent her assurance in turn, and her competence steadily developed. With the summer Marchmont home received generous gifts such as her father had made at the beginning, and she was called upon to preserve quantities of fruit. She counted hundreds of jars that she had filled. One day she turned to find Miss Bilbrough regarding her thoughtfully.

"You're a square peg in a round hole, Lizzie," she said. The phrase was still unhackneyed, quite new to Elizabeth. It seemed to mean only that she had failed to meet expectations, and her face flushed. But Miss Bilbrough went on with quiet earnestness. "You've a mind as intelligent as your brother's; and yet because you are a woman, you still think that such work is your fulfilment. You insist that you must do it voluntarily, that you can accept no pay. Then let me send you for a year to the Women's Medical College, pay the expenses I know you can't meet.''

Elizabeth could only stammer her thanks—''Miss Bilbrough was the first real lady I had ever known,'' she would recall, ''and I loved her.''

She wrote to John Grace, telling him of her happiness in this opportunity that had seemed only the most remote of dreams; and his reply startled her from any easy acceptance of their casual friendship. He urged her to abandon this difficult, foolish course for a woman, and to marry him instead. She answered that she would not consider the choice and that his letter had only troubled her. She must give attention to her duties.

When he wrote again, after an interval of some weeks, he had resumed the earlier manner of their correspondence, with only a note that he was yielding to her wishes, and he begged her to continue writing to him, for letters from her were all that gave direction to his wandering life.

She answered from Kingston, telling him with light friendship once more, of her studies and her associates in the College.

Four

Every student enrolled in the Women's Medical College and registered at Queen's was familiar with the story of strong opposition there to women in the field of Medicine. The Faculty at Queen's had been established in 1854, and was reorganized in 1866 as the Royal College of Physicians and Surgeons, affiliated with Queen's University, a proud distinction that it retained until 1891, when it resumed its former status.

In the summer of 1880, ''a course of lectures for women exclusively'' had been established; and then six women were admitted to the regular session of 1881-82, though with a separate dissecting room, and a classroom adjacent to the general one where they might take jurisprudence, obstetrics, anatomy and physiology separately. It was in the following year's session that the men students sent their ultimatum to the Faculty, stating that if women were to continue at the College, the men would go in a body to the University of Trinity College in Toronto.

Of the small group of women who were then in their third year of studies, and who experienced the full force of that unjust and deliberately instigated revolt, two became instructors in the Women's Medical College—a College that seemed the best solution to a troubled situation, though a similar one for women was opened at the same time in Toronto. Some of the professors at Queen's and many of the townspeople had been active in the

Photograph taken in Kingston (1888) of the class of '91 of the Women's Medical College, in affiliation with Queen's University.
Standing, left to right: Janet Murray, Margaret O'Hara, Nell Skimmin.
Seated, left to right: Janet Weir, Elizabeth Scott (Matheson),
Jean Sinclair (Mackay).
At front, left to right: Mary Birmingham, Mary MacCallum (Scott).

---

establishment of the Kingston College in rooms on the third floor of their large City Hall.

In 1887, there were about thirty women enrolled, eight of them in the class of '91. They went together to Queen's for classes in chemistry and botany, but all the classes in Medicine were conducted in the rooms at City Hall, under professors from the Royal College of Physicians and Surgeons, who set the examinations for men and women alike.

The girls in the class of '91 usually met at the street door of City Hall, where Nell Skimmin, as their leader, would marshall them with her clear laughing voice—"Heads up, girls, and heels down"—to begin their climb up and up, seventy steps in all to the top floor.

One member of that class was invariably late, whether to the assembly at the Women's College, or at Queen's where the women made a practice of meeting early, to take their places quietly in the front row of the lecture theatre. She was Mary Birmingham, a lovely brunette, and the unquestioned beauty of their class.

25

At Queen's, she would pause for a moment, alone at the top of the steps in the theatre, before she began her calm descent, in the silence that always fell. If the professor had begun his lecture, that too would wait, for every head would turn to watch the lovely girl. Then the rhythmic stamp of the men's feet would begin, growing louder and louder, keeping time with each unhurried graceful step she took, only the soft colouring of her face giving the least indication that she heard them.

One day, however, as she took her place beside Elizabeth, she murmured something; and a man behind tapped Elizabeth's shoulder. "What did Miss Birmingham say?" The answer was unhesitating. He stood at once, turned to face the tiers of students, raised his arm for their attention, and declared solemnly, "Gentlemen, Miss Birmingham says NUTS."

For the girls in their classes there was always the consciousness that they must exert themselves to counteract discrimination against women, to disprove the fatuous argument that their minds were incapable of intense and prolonged study. They encouraged one another to excel. Elizabeth could rejoice that in the spring examinations she tied with one of the men in botany, each receiving 100%. But for her the competitive rivalry lost its edge in her brother's frank appreciation of her achievements.

There was also the easy comradeship of her boarding-house, where she was the only girl with Tom and three other men, students in Arts, Theology and Law. Partly because of that association, but more because it saved time and effort, she had her hair cut like a boy's. It was dark-brown hair, soft and fine, not easily worn in any style that the age considered flattering. But the boy's cut suited her, and she kept to it for years.

She followed her brother's example by adding their mother's maiden name to the single name given in baptism; for neither "Thomas" nor "Elizabeth" was unusual in the least, and there were many Scotts at Queen's. He became Thomas Beckett Scott, and she Elizabeth Beckett Scott.

It was this happy relationship with her brother that lent the whole year its shining quality. Together they joined the Student Volunteer Movement for Foreign Missions when John Raleigh Mott came to Queen's on his tour of eastern universities.

When he was eighty years of age, Dr. Mott would receive a Nobel prize for Peace in recognition of his long service in international church and missionary movements; but he was only twenty-three in that spring of 1888, recently graduated from Cornell University at Ithaca, N.Y., and student secretary of the International Committee of the Young Men's Christian

Association. He was already a practised and eloquent speaker, and his purpose was to organize the Student Volunteer Movement for Foreign Missions. The years that closed the nineteenth century were the golden age of missionary enthusiasm, and students crowded his meetings.

Two of Elizabeth's classmates, Jean Sinclair and Mary MacCallum, sat with her and Tom; but when the four walked home through the quiet streets, Jean and Elizabeth went together, while Tom walked with Mary. Hearing their low voices, and Mary's amused laughter, Elizabeth knew that not all their talk was of missionary endeavour, and that Tom's wit was set to win the girl. That she was worth the effort could not quite restrain the pang of jealousy that Elizabeth felt.

Mary, the daughter of a Congregational minister, was one of the childhood friends whom Ralph Connor would remember when he wrote *Glengarry School Days*. She had entered nursing first, graduating from Harper Hospital in Detroit before she was twenty. Her record was outstanding, and she had been persuaded to enter Medical College, assured that between sessions she would find ready employment at Harper Hospital. The doctors would even hold operations over for a few days until she could be there to assist; and she would hurry to the train from her final examinations, in order to begin her work early the next morning.

Tom had resolved that he would enter Medicine when he had completed Arts and Theology, financing his course with work each summer as supervisor for Marchmont Home. Miss Bilbrough's concern for the welfare of the boys and girls in her charge went far beyond any quick placement on Canadian farms. She recognized Tom's continuing interest, his understanding sympathy for her charges together with his grasp of the conditions to which they must adjust; and she paid him a generous salary for his supervision of their progress.

Five

In that one definite respect, all the men had a clear advantage—their earning power during the summers. Elizabeth's own small savings from four years of teaching had almost vanished; and lacking Miss Bilbrough's help, she would have to teach for at least a year before she could return to Medical College. But while she was still at Kingston, she could take advantage of the summer classes that Queen's offered, and she enrolled in second-year chemistry and botany, completing both classes successfully.

The school at Poplar Point accepted her application without hesitation;

and then she tendered her resignation within a few weeks. It was accepted with regret on both parts, for Elizabeth had settled eagerly into the work —children and parents alike happy to receive her once more. The chairman, however, felt honoured in granting her release, requested as it was in person by Dr. John M. King, the esteemed principal of Manitoba College.

Dr. King had driven from Winnipeg to interview Elizabeth on behalf of the Presbyterian Board of Missions in Toronto, whose mission field in Central India had appealed for teachers. That Board knew of her only as a member of the Student Volunteer Movement at Queen's, but her classmate, Jean Sinclair, had recommended her, and had herself agreed to abandon studies in Medicine.

Elizabeth left hurriedly for an interview with the Board in Toronto, and John Grace's letter came to her there. He had learned of the new development only when his sister Christiana's note had reached him, for Elizabeth had not stopped to write.

He pleaded with her now to cancel the agreement and return to her previous decision to study Medicine. He would pay for her entire course, if she would promise even to consider marrying him later. A year earlier, he had tried to prevent those studies, but now anything was preferable to this sudden decision to leave Canada, under contract for seven years. If she went to India, she would surely be lost to him forever, and he could not bear that. She was all that meant anything in his life.

There was only one answer that she could make. She was going to India. More than that, he could have no part in her life now; her new work would require all her attention, and his letters disturbed her too much. They must end. She would answer no more of them; and she asked him not to write to her again. When she sealed her letter, she knew there would be no answer. She could forget him. But it would have been easier for her if each new adventure in the weeks that followed had not brought the same quick reaction: ''I must tell John Matheson when I write.''

She sailed with Jean Sinclair in November, arriving in Britain with time only for a brief visit with Jean's people in Ayrshire before they embarked at London on one of the Pacific and Orient steamships, to arrive in Bombay on New Year's Day, 1889.

While crossing the Red Sea, Elizabeth experienced a fever that she thought was caused by too much heat and sun, but that the Mission doctor at Indore soon recognized as malaria. Steadily she lost the rounded plumpness of girlhood, in recurring bouts of fever that even the refreshment of holidays in Simla could not quite abate. But she loved her work, and made progress in

28

Elizabeth on Abdul at Neemuch in Central India (1890).

her lessons in Hindustani, acquiring enough competency to assume much of the responsibility when she went to the smaller mission at Neemuch.

Letters had an importance that they would never lose again for Elizabeth. Hers went out to all the members of her family in turn, the swift sentences running across page after page of thin paper, in her singularly strong hand-writing. She told of her progress in the language and of how she was adapting to the work in school and bazaar; she gave details of the simple furnishings that she and her companion worker had chosen for their bungalow; she spoke of tennis games and her developing skill; and with great happiness she described the lovely bay stallion that she had bought, and her delight in riding and driving him.

He was called Abdul; and he was supposed to be "spavined", she wrote, and that was why the British officer had sold him. But what did that mean? she asked her farming brothers. All she could remember was "Spavin" Shillinglaw, when they were children at Burnbrae. Abdul seemed quite sound in wind and limb. She'd match him in a race with any horse her brother Will might have.

Very early one morning before the heat of the day, she took Abdul out, while his groom, the syce, ran at her stirrup. But that meant too easy a trot. She wanted something faster, was eager to try Abdul's pace. The syce could wait for them at the bridge, and they would take a longer, more round-about way. She heard the bugle sound at the parade-ground, far across the river; and Abdul pricked his ears, reminding her that he had been a cavalry horse. His pace quickened. And then, sharp and clear, the bugle came again, sounding the charge—and he was away. To hold him was impossible. All she could do was cling to that foolish side-saddle, the skirts of her smart riding-habit streaming behind. Abdul left the road, and was racing at full gallop straight towards the river and that far bugle. But the syce had heard the call too, knew what it could mean, and was racing on foot from the bridge, along the bank, to meet them at the very edge of the river. He leaped and caught Abdul's bridle, seemed to hang there for one fearful moment before the well-trained horse finally stopped.

When there were longer intervals between her letters, she blamed the pressure of her work; or, if her writing seemed to waver, the paper or the pen was at fault. Not until late in her second year, did she admit to her family that she was often fevered, had little energy for work or play, that to drive Abdul was easier than riding. Still, she was certain that she could overcome it all. But the doctor decided otherwise, and wrote to the Board of Missions. Early in 1891, they ordered her home to Canada.

She sailed in February, and Jean Sinclair accompanied her to the port of Bombay. The parting distressed them both, though they cheered one another with the hopeful insistence that when Elizabeth completed her studies in Medicine, the Board would let her return to India as a doctor.

Then at Kingston, when Elizabeth attended the graduation of the class of '91, there was the same cheerful encouragement. If she could quickly regain her strength, she might even be back in Kingston before Tom finished his course in Medicine.

Mary MacCallum had left Queen's to take her final year at the Woman's Medical College of the New York Infirmary for Women and Children, and had been drawn into settlement work on the lower East Side of that city. Tom was confident, however, that they would be married when he graduated in his turn, and that they would serve together in some far mission.

Jim Scott had married Jennie Henderson of Cook's Creek, and they were living in New Westminster. While Elizabeth was still in India, Jim had written, telling her that John Matheson had called at their home. He was establishing himself as a building contractor in the town, and had a good name in the trades; but there had been an interval of two years in the mountains of British Columbia and Idaho, and there were stories of his life in mining camps that made Jennie's welcome a bit uncertain. Many of his associates in the town were from the rougher element, and his life was certainly not the sober church-going one that Jim and Jennie led.

Still, he had been inquiring for Elizabeth, and Jim had promised that he would tell her. Matheson was not easily discouraged, it seemed. He had called on their sister Janet too—again perhaps as a matter of course since her husband, Alex MacKay, was in the lumbering business in Vancouver.

Six

To Elizabeth, in India, the news of John Matheson recalled the strange wandering life that had touched hers briefly—and was gone. In Canada, her only concern was to win back her strength, and then return to her studies in Medicine. Her parents were in North Dakota, on a farm near Tyner, with her youngest brother. She would stay with them, then teach—perhaps in Manitoba—before she entered College again.

It was in June that her brother came from the Tyner post office with a letter for her, and she recognized Matheson's once familiar writing. His letter spoke first of his joy in the news that she had returned from India. To her, that had meant the discouraging end to adventurous work, and his words conveyed a lack of understanding that she resented deeply. She read the continuing pages, as from an intruding stranger, and she answered the letter indifferently with trite, meaningless phrases.

She was in happier spirits a few days later when she read it again, and realized that the resentment she had felt had its roots only in her own dejection at the time. Now, the whole letter came suddenly to life, the words full of meaning as he told her of the wondrous experience that had come to him.

It had happened before he even knew that she was returning from India, while she was crossing the Atlantic in March. With some companions, he had been wandering along streets in the roughest section of New Westminster, looking for any idle amusement. They came, in the same spirit, to a meeting held by two Methodist revivalists from Toronto. And in that crowded hall, John Matheson had experienced the amazing force of true conversion.

Others might say that his conversion was only a return to the influences of early boyhood, the result of all the concern expressed by his God-fearing people, and Elizabeth's own rejection of him. But he alone had known the reality, had felt the full revitalizing force of change in his whole attitude to life.

And Elizabeth, as she read the words afresh, found every real barrier between herself and John Grace swept aside, knew the strength of love that his letters and his own constancy had often faintly stirred, felt all resistance melt away. With tears on her face, she wrote to him, humbly begging forgiveness for the indifference of her previous letter, trying to explain the conflict of six years within herself, using for the first time the tender words of love. "I was blind, my darling, but you know it was not wilfully."

She would not trust the letter to her brother's casual hands, and rode to the post office herself, where she made careful inquiries and knew that she could not expect a reply for ten days at least. But it was only five days later that her brother handed her a letter addressed in the familiar writing, and she knew that it must have been written in answer to her first, on the very day that she had posted her second. She read the carefully phrased sentences—only kindness there, acknowledgement of the difference that lay between them in years and in the ways of life that the years of each had compassed. It was unlikely, he wrote, that they would ever meet again, but he would remember her always.

When the afternoon of the tenth day came, the air was sultry, the sky ominous. Her brother and father were working four horse-teams in the field, and there was only a spirited mare in the stable, one that she had been expressly forbidden to ride, unused as it was to side-saddle and full riding skirts, and terrified as well of storms. Elizabeth saddled it, however, and rode with the easy assurance of her training in India. At the post office she found the awaited letter, and read it eagerly, her heart beating with happiness from the first words. She tucked it into a deep pocket of her riding habit, and mounted quickly, her excitement as high as the mare's when the storm broke.

In the meantime, her father and brother had hurried from the field, and Will learned of his sister's venture. There was time only to pull the harness from one of the heavy work-horses and ride it down the road to meet Elizabeth. He was certain she could not control the mare. When they met on a narrow stretch of the road, he barred the way, insisting that she must ride his horse, bareback or not, and he would manage both mare and side-saddle. He had expected that Elizabeth would be terrified by the wild ride she had had, but she was laughing and exultant as they raced for shelter from the flash and thunder of the storm.

32

The letter had read: "My darling, this name that I never called another woman on earth, I did suspect that you were troubled, but how could a man who has been among women as little as I, be expected to read a woman's heart. For myself, I will say this. My love for you never has changed and never can, whatever may come between us. The love of a man my age is altogether different from the passion of a boy of twenty. . . . In these past months, I have found the pearl of great price, and now I have learned that the one woman I love above all women, loves even poor old wandering Grace."

It was a long letter, touching upon the years that were past, upon the months of adjustment and change for him during the spring, upon the plans that he was making to see her again.

During the next few weeks, his letters came frequently. When she referred again to the letter that she bitterly regretted, he wrote: "I am at this moment thanking God that it was written. Do you think that my darling would ever have lifted the screen and shown me her heart? Do you think that ever the *woman* could have overcome 'Miss Scott' and *my* Lizzie have shown me that she loved me, if that letter had not been written. I believe that I might have gone to my grave and never known that. My darling, my darling, how much happiness I owe that letter, how proud a man I am to know that you came out of the trial as a *woman* and showed me love that is not sentimental dross, that is worth a man's life, worth waiting for these six years. God bless you and keep you safe, and bring you speedily to me, your lover till death."

He told her how he cherished her letters, keeping them always on his person, except when engaged in work that was so far removed from his feeling for her that it seemed a desecration to carry them.

With three other men—including her brother—he had rented a hall for the work to which he gave all his free hours. "Last night," he wrote, "the place was crowded with people who never see the inside of a church. Let me picture to you the locality in the lowest and most degraded part of the city, on a narrow street, the one part of the building we are in occupied by two coloured—I won't say what kind of women—and immediately opposite us, sixty feet away, two houses filled with white women of the same character as the others—the whole place reeking with profanity, and whisky, and debauchery of every kind—chinamen, blacks, indians and whites—men and women of the worst possible class. My own Lizzie, can you picture John Grace addressing a prayer meeting in such a place? That is just what I did. And God was with me. I did it with the most perfect coolness, just glad of the chance. I saw some of my old associates were listening while I spoke, some out on the street, some in the house, and to them I especially addressed myself. That was my first attempt to preach the word of God, although two Sundays ago I had spoken a few words of advice to the white men who were mingling with the chinamen in their Mission."

He wrote of individuals he had helped. "Last night I took to my room a poor man who attempted to commit suicide in the evening, a poor degraded drunkard, brother of a man who was mayor of Winnipeg. He had been on a fearful spree for days, got the d.t.'s as we call it, and was going to destroy himself. He was prevented, and instead of being put in jail was turned over to me, into whose hands he willingly placed himself. This may be the turning point of his life. I think it can be."

More often, he wrote about their own plans, which were still uncertain; and for that reason he begged, "Keep all this in your heart, a secret till we meet, so that if it should happen that my fondest hopes should not be realized, no living soul can scoff at my disappointment."

He urged Elizabeth to come to her sister's home in Vancouver, and in August she was on her way, telegraphing him from Winnipeg. He had hoped to meet her at North Bend on the Fraser River, when the train stopped so that passengers might have their breakfast on the last day of a long journey. That proved impossible for him, and a telegram awaited her there instead, assuring her that when the train was within forty miles of New Westminster, he would board it.

He had written, "I am as impatient as a boy could be, but, my darling, I cannot help almost dreading our meeting, nervous as to what the decision may be. That is only human. Remember, my Lizzie, I am much older, and also an older-looking man than I was six years ago. I got very grey this winter. Perhaps you may not love me when you see me. I leave you to judge, when we meet. I would consider it unmanly of me to try to bind you to anything until then. If, after you have seen me, you are of the same opinion still, you will tell me. If not, why still, God bless you. I ask you—no, I do not ask you. I command you—do this as unto God, and do not consider my feelings. I would a thousand times rather see my darling happy in another man's arms than unhappy in mine, even though it broke my heart. Let your judgment, your heart, and our God decide. And oh, may God bless you and guide you all your life, whatever the decision may be."

She waited tensely as the train slowed to a halt for one passenger whom the conductor greeted cheerfully as an old acquaintance; but when he came to sit beside her, all nervousness went, and they talked together simply as friends who had not met for six years. He would leave her again at New

John Matheson (*c*. 1890).

Westminster to avoid any speculation on her brother-in-law's part should they arrive in Vancouver together; but that afternoon, he assured her, he would come to Vancouver, and call on her sister, possibly take the two of them for a drive about that city.

When he came, however, he had learned that every carriage was taking part in a civic procession. He suggested a rowboat instead, on Burrard Inlet, and was not disappointed when Janet refused. She was six months pregnant, and having lost her first child would take no undue chance. In any case, she hated the water. But Elizabeth was free to go, and it would be a pleasant outing after the long train journey. This was more than they had hoped to achieve easily.

They rowed across the Inlet to where the wreck of the old Hudson's Bay Company ship *The Beaver* was stranded; they scrambled over and about it; then walked through Stanley Park, still testing their uncertain commitment.

Elizabeth said hesitantly that it might be possible for her to return even that year to her studies at Queen's, for Alex MacKay had mentioned the possibility of a loan. That brought John Grace to an abrupt stop, an unexpectedly jealous note in his voice, and sharp disappointment. He had told her how diminished were his own financial resources. Her earlier refusal to marry him had only spurred his recklessness with money, and during the six months past there had not been a plea for help that he had refused. If she was determined to continue her studies, then he would finance them, not another man. Only marry him first. He could not bear the separation otherwise.

The intensity of his feeling moved her deeply, overcoming the last reluctance to abandon those studies entirely. Now she told him that she would not return to Medical College, not ever. She would be content and happy simply to be his wife, and she would marry him as soon as it was possible.

He was wearing a ring, a wide band of gold from the Saskatchewan River, and he tried that on her finger, as their engagement ring. First he wanted to have it engraved, not with their names but with the name "Ruth" and the numerals 1-17. She could repeat the words of that verse from the Bible with him from memory: "The Lord do so to me, and more also, if aught but death part thee and me."

In her own happiness and her conviction as to the wisdom of their decision, Elizabeth was not prepared for the opposition that she met from both her brother and her sister. It was John Matheson's age that troubled Jim particularly. "He'll only leave you a widow, with a family of red-headed boys." Janet's attitude struck Elizabeth to the heart, for it revealed the change that personal bitterness had made in a sister whom she had admired from earliest childhood. "Give this John Matheson six months and he'll be back to his old ways. I'll have no part in it."

She kept to her word, refusing even to turn her skill at dressmaking to Elizabeth's wedding preparations, or to show the least interest. It was a neighbour, Mrs. Taylor, who offered to help make the wedding-dress of soft French grey, and who went with Elizabeth to the Presbyterian manse on December 8 for the marriage service. One of John Matheson's friends came with him from New Westminster. There were no other witnesses, both Janet and Jim refusing to attend.

The two women were early at the manse, and Dr. McLaren received them courteously, talking pleasantly to Mrs. Taylor while Elizabeth sat quietly. Then he looked at his watch. "I'll have to ask you to leave. I've a wedding in ten minutes." Mrs. Taylor commented drily, "Send this young lady away, Dr. McLaren, and you'll have an angry man on your hands."

John Grace had acquired land some forty miles from New Westminster, which he described as "a ranch", and where he was building a house; but its completion had to wait upon other work, and they lived in the furnished rooms that he had rented in town.

He would not take her into the area where he had rented the hall, but she did accompany him to other meetings. She knew of the taunts that he had had to face, but these were passing with the months of steady resolution on his part. She thought that they could never have been too deliberate, for he had always been well liked; but there would be apprehension on the part of doubters. Should there be any reversion to the old "Roaring Jack", he could have the readiest pair of fists in town. They knew of many bouts, and had heard particularly of one in the ring at a mining camp in the States, when he had "put on the gloves" with champion John L. Sullivan himself.

Any jeer that Elizabeth over-heard, she learned to disregard as he did, but comments about him were much more often of his kindness and his generosity. She treasured these, knowing that few of them were intended for her ears, a stranger as she was to many. Now and then, a comment would amuse her. One woman, speaking directly to Elizabeth, remarked, "He says that he was born in Manitoba, but he's the first red-headed half-breed I've ever seen."

Seven

Even before the year ended, John Matheson had made his decision. He would give up his work as a contractor, and would volunteer for mission service wherever he might be useful. Since he regarded himself as Presbyterian, and it was for that Church that Elizabeth had been a missionary, he applied there first. He was told that, for a man of his age, and without any theological training, there would be few openings. The Methodists could only say that there might be a possibility that they could use him among the Indians of the Naas River; and they would let him know.

Edward Matheson, of his own volition, had spoken of his brother's decision to the Bishop of Calgary and Saskatchewan. Bishop Pinkham remembered the young man who had taught St. James parish school more than twenty years before; and recalled Elizabeth as a new teacher, when he had been superintendent of education in Manitoba. He spoke to Samuel Pritchard Matheson, then Canon of St. John's Cathedral in Winnipeg. He was reminded that John Matheson was closely associated with the Anglican Church through his mother's family, the Pritchards; and that to serve as an Anglican might be less remarkable than his decision to be a missionary—if that were sincere. For with S.P. Matheson the doubt remained—"I thought it could be just another of John Grace's tricks."

If Edward Matheson had any doubts, his affection for his brother overrode them quite. He knew of his fluency in Cree and his wide acquaintance among the people of the Saskatchewan; he knew John Grace's unquestioned ability. The Bishop agreed. He wrote, asking Matheson to return to the Territories as an Anglican missionary in the Diocese of Saskatchewan. He could offer him a post as teacher on Sekaskooch Indian Reserve, a few miles north-west of Fort Pitt, on the old Fort Carlton-Fort Edmonton trail.

It would be expected, of course, that both he and his wife should be confirmed members of the Church, since he would serve as catechist and lay-reader to the several Indian Reserves that were the charge of St. Barnabas Mission at Onion Lake. The Bishop would also outline studies that Matheson was to follow, in preparation for eventual ordination; but these were to be undertaken together with his work as teacher and catechist, for it was never intended that he should enter any theological college.

Because of his half-commitment to the Methodists, John Matheson answered the Bishop uncertainly, giving him the reason. The reply to that went directly to the heart of the matter. "I call you," the Bishop wrote, "not to serve any one Church, but to serve the Lord."

"I've earned a good living serving the Devil," John Grace remarked to Elizabeth. "I can earn a better one serving the Lord." The salary he was offered was $300 a year; and he and Elizabeth accepted that as they later accepted its increase to a maximum of $600, their confidence lying not so much in their own ability, which they took for granted, as in the assurance they felt much more strongly that "He who hath begun a good work in you, will perform it to the end."

Elizabeth had never known better health or greater happiness. Springtime was in both their hearts, as well as all around them; for they knew that when the bright summer of the country that John Grace loved blazed into autumn along the old Fort Carlton trail, she would bear his child.

While they were making their plans to leave British Columbia, her parents came to live in New Westminster. The resistance of her sister and brother to the marriage had moderated even before John Grace charmed Elizabeth's mother. To break through James Scott's quiet reserve needed more time, but his attitude was understanding, and Elizabeth was thankful. When he came to say good-bye, both knew that they might never see one another again. He brought her a gift, four five-dollar gold pieces. No rich dowry could have meant more to her than this from her quiet, hard-working father. In her first winter at the Mission, she would have to use three of those pieces, but the fourth she kept always, having the word "Father" engraved upon it, that it might never be spent.

She left New Westminster with John Grace in May, going as far east as Winnipeg to visit his people, before returning west to travel from Regina to Saskatoon by the Qu'Appelle-Long Lake-Saskatchewan railway. This line extended on to Prince Albert and had been completed in 1890, the trestle bridge at Saskatoon John Matheson's final contract in railroad building. Saskatoon was still no more than half-a-dozen houses that were either stores or stopping-places for freighters and stage-coach drivers and such travellers as themselves.

It was late in the day when they arrived at the station, and John Grace took her to the stopping-place he considered the better of the two. There was little to choose between them, he warned her, but when they entered their room, the sharp acrid scent of bedbugs repelled her. He gave only a quick glance at the iron bedstead and straw-filled mattress across its wooden slats, then stripped a blanket from it, shook it vigorously, and spread it on the floor.

"We'll try this," he said, and lay down; but Elizabeth sat beside him, her skirts wrapped tightly about her knees, tense in the dim light, hearing the faint scratch and fall of searching crawlers. He rose and drew her to her feet. "It's a fine warm night. Let's try the river bank." He shook the blanket again, and swung it over his arm.

They escaped into the star-lit beauty of the wide prairie night, and walked along the river. He spread the blanket and sat beside her, smoking his pipe, studying the dark shadows of the trestle bridge, telling her of the celebrations when the first work-train had reached the hamlet on the east side of the river in May of 1890.

She listened drowsily until sleep overcame her, and when she wakened the day was only dawning, but he was standing impatiently. "It's light enough," he insisted, and took her arm to guide her along the bank. She waited while he ran his eye along the timbered structure of the bridge, and then walked over it beside him, stepping cautiously from one tie to the next. He tested each appraisingly, stopping to consider the trestles, the murmuring river below them reflecting in its murky waters their figures and the bridge.

He was smiling and relaxed, any uneasiness he may have felt in returning to the Territories quite gone. She was thankful. In British Columbia, the atmosphere had often been charged with emotionalism, a straining after piety that disturbed her less demonstrative nature, and that she feared could submerge the lively zest and spirit that she loved. In Winnipeg, she had noticed his frequent laughter and robust humour. His pipe had appeared again, and there were occasions when she suspected a convivial drink with old friends. She was not troubled by that. In fact, she welcomed this return to his more normal life, quite confident of the strength and sincerity of his conversion.

They walked on through the sleeping hamlet on the east bank, and then returned across the bridge. Smoke was rising from the stove-pipes of the kitchen at the stopping-place. Elizabeth found a clean towel in her bag, and rinsed the common basin at the pump in the yard before they washed. Breakfast would be thick oatmeal porridge, with syrup, fat bacon, bread and strong tea.

At seven o'clock the stage-coach left for Battleford. It was a two-seated democrat, with room for the mail-bags and some of their luggage; but the heavier articles, their trunks and boxes would be freighted by wagon to Battleford. There they could buy what supplies they might need, though Elizabeth knew how limited those purchases must be, restricted by their own slim resources and the further cost of freighting another hundred miles to

40

Onion Lake. One wagon-load was all they could permit themselves. For the rest, their own ingenuity had to suffice.

Leeson and Scott had the contract then for the mails, which included passenger service and arrangements for stopping-houses at twenty-five to thirty-mile distances, a long enough drive in winter weather. The recently surveyed trail from Saskatoon led north-west towards the elbow of the North Saskatchewan River, and then along the south bank until it came to the crossing of the Battle River.

The first day's drive was to the telegraph station at Henrietta, where the log building was comfortable, offering decent enough accommodation for the night. At noon on the second day, the stage reached "Charlie, the Swede's", and here the passengers had dinner and the horses were changed. Charlie was a friendly talkative person, hired for his skill with horses, able to shoe them or to mend harness and wagons, a handy man in the lonely business of mail-carrying through country where there was still no settlement.

On the second night, the stop was at Baljeanie, named for a daughter of the Warden family, in a farm house where there was accommodation for travellers and as good meals as anywhere in the country. Then, starting early in the third morning, the stage reached Battleford at noon.

In 1892, when mail could go twice a week from the railway at Saskatoon to Battleford, it seemed a remarkable improvement in communication to the people of that town, accustomed as they had been in earlier years to mail only once in three weeks from Winnipeg.

Even that name "Winnipeg" became "Fort Garry" as John Grace recalled the years when he had carried the first government mails to the Territories. Battleford then was simply the ford across the Battle, where conflicts between Cree and Blackfoot were still part of living memory, and the Hudson's Bay Company had no permanent post on this stretch of the Saskatchewan River between Fort Carlton and Fort Pitt.

James McKay of Deer Lodge on the Assiniboine had had the contract then, and John Grace had run the first mail in January of 1875, on snowshoes, with a dog-team, from Fort Garry by way of the frozen Narrows of Lake Manitoba to Fort Livingstone, the newly-built barracks of the North-West Mounted Police in the Swan River district. It was to be used as headquarters until Fort Macleod and then Fort Walsh proved more central in the international troubles with whisky-smugglers and Sitting Bull's Sioux Indians. Fort Livingstone was to be the seat of government too, until Battleford was chosen.

It was only that one winter mail that was carried the first year as far as Fort Livingstone, more than three hundred miles. The Hudson's Bay Company's "winter packet" still went out from Fort Pelly and Fort Carlton; and the Police had their own courier service between stations. Then the next winter, John Grace had carried the mails to Fort Edmonton, running in all some five thousand miles of winter mail-carrying between Fort Pelly, Fort Carlton and Fort Edmonton.

There was no passenger service then. Anyone who travelled with the mail-carrier, went on snowshoes too. Nor were there stopping-houses, just camps in the snow, frozen fish for the dogs, and pemmican for the runner —good nourishing stuff. With that to sustain him, he had made a record run of six and a half days from Fort Pelly to Fort Garry, though it was springtime then, and the trails and river crossings bad. One of the young Inksters from Kildonan was with him, and they had had to carry the packs themselves.

In the summer of 1876, the full contract for the mails was put into effect—seventeen trips a year, at three-week intervals, between Fort Garry and Fort Edmonton, with horses and buckboard in the summer and dogs still for winter travelling. There were two carriers for that, John Grace for one more year before he turned to freighting, and John Todd; one of them from Edmonton, which Matheson chose for his base, and the other from Winnipeg. They met at Fort Pelly that year, but later Battleford became the exchange point and Todd established himself there.

Battleford got its first mail late in 1876, when the telegraph line had been extended that far, and the government buildings were being constructed. But then the southern route was chosen for the Canadian Pacific Railway, and Regina became the capital instead, and headquarters for the North-West Mounted Police as well. As the railroad crossed the plains, there could be more frequent mail-service for the Saskatchewan with horses in winter or summer, first from Qu'Appelle and then from Swift Current to Battleford.

Now, in 1892, ninety miles of summer trail from Saskatoon to Battleford, with bridges over Eagle Creek and the Battle River, seemed by comparison easy travelling.

Eight

For Elizabeth, the memories of that trip, the details of the trail and of the stopping-places were to merge into recollections of twenty-five years more of such journeyings, until only the truly exceptional would be remembered.

The coming to Battleford meant more to both of them. Here John Grace's younger brother, Edward Matheson, served as incumbent of St. George's, with Bresaylor and Saskatoon also in his charge. Only a few weeks before their coming, he had married Josephine Raymond, a member of the staff at the Indian Industrial School, from London, Ontario. Music and art had been part of her gentler life in the east, and their home reflected this, and the quiet orderliness that was Edward Matheson's way.

It was this marked contrast to John Grace that most impressed Elizabeth. The bond between the brothers was strong, for all the difference in temperament, and they rejoiced in this new unity of work and life. Physically they were not too unalike, though Edward lacked two inches of John's six feet. His red hair curled as crisply, over a brow as high, but it was more distinctly red than John's auburn, and the eyes beneath were brown. His short full beard seemed to blaze in the sunlight, while John's clipped one was grey now. There, however, the resemblance seemed to end. John's casual dress was that of any other westerner, and Edward's precise clerical attire was carefully tended. It was not only that it fitted him neatly; he seemed formed to wear it.

Their voices had the same rich tones, but Edward expressed himself with the slow precision of a thoughtful studious man. He was punctilious in any duty, in the arrangement of services at the three points in his charge, in his

Edward Matheson (*standing*), his sister Eliza Lamb (*at right*), his half-sister Letitia Cunningham, and his friend at Emmanuel College, the Rev. Arthur Wright. (Winnipeg, 1890.)

regular attendance at synods and meetings, or in the most trivial routine. During fifteen years in the Diocese of Saskatchewan, he had proved a selfless dedication that would continue to the end of his life.

Elizabeth could be thankful that her husband had this steadfast example, even while she cherished the qualities that made him John Grace. Life with him could be much livelier, and full of the unexpected.

With her new sister-in-law, she was not quite at ease. Elizabeth's height and strong free carriage still lent her grace, and she knew that she was lovely in her health and happiness; but she was seven months pregnant, and an embarrassment to a bride accustomed to all the primness of that time. Careful conventions and rules never had been truly a part of Elizabeth's life, and seemed only tiresome to her. She longed to be in her own home; and John Grace was even more impatient as the days passed.

Word at Battleford was simply that the Reverend Isaac Taylor was not ready to leave St. Barnabas Mission. It had been understood that he was leaving the Diocese to return to England, but now it seemed that only his wife and children would go. He hoped to be assigned to another mission in the Diocese.

In any case, he would let the Mathesons know. Mail service between Onion Lake and Battleford, however, was only once every three weeks. A telegraph station operated at Fort Pitt, and that was twelve miles from Onion Lake. Even urgent telegrams might wait for the appearance of a casual Indian rider; but word came finally, after much prompting, that Taylor would follow the plan that Matheson proposed. They would meet on July 12 at Fort Pitt, exchanging conveyances on opposite banks of the river.

The river, as John Matheson knew well, could be crossed with comparative ease a little distance below the old fort, where a sand-bar divided the stream, and a heavy flat-bottomed boat was kept for the deeper channel. Otherwise, Matheson would have had to cross as the cart brigades had in earlier days, and that was a long-drawn-out process. To exchange conveyances in this case could be simpler.

He planned every detail of the familiar trip. To freight their goods as far as the south bank at Fort Pitt, he had engaged another Taylor—Peter Taylor of Bresaylor, one of the three principal families of that settlement, Bremner, Sayer and Taylor, from whose surnames ''Bresaylor'' was derived, the only settlement between Battleford and Onion Lake. Peter Taylor had agreed to drive a wagon loaded with their goods, and supply another team and a buckboard that John Matheson would drive.

They left Battleford in the early morning of July 10, driving north-west still, following the course of the North Saskatchewan. At Saskatoon, it had been the South Branch, but to Elizabeth this other would never be the North Branch, but the Saskatchewan itself, the great river of the fur-traders.

They went through most beautiful parkland country, bright with flowers, sweet with the scent of wolf-willow and wild roses. In any coulee, in any hollow that escaped the winds and the ever constant threat of prairie fires, bushes of saskatoons, chokecherries, and pincherries were ripening. On the river banks, the raspberries would soon be sweet, and in the warm sun-dried grass wild strawberries reddened.

After long hours of jolting in the rough buckboard, Elizabeth considered a five o'clock morning start quite early enough; but when they camped at "the Big Gully" the second evening, John Grace said, "There'll be no more of this pampering. You're on the trail now, my Bessie, and you may as well know it. Three o'clock tomorrow, with the sun, and if you're not out of this tent by ten minutes past, it's coming down around you."

She wakened to the first song of birds in the earliest light of northern summer. She was alone in the tent. There was the scent of wood-smoke from the fire outside, the shuffling thump of hobbled horses driven in from the night's grazing, the sound of men's voices. Then suddenly, the tent sagged. "I said ten minutes past three." She scrambled from under the tent as it fell. "Tea's ready." Only farther along the trail would there be a stop for breakfast.

It was still morning when they came to the steep southern bank and saw the river far below them. The northern banks, more than four hundred yards across the river, rose hundreds of feet, the grassy uplands sweeping as far as the eye could see, with only an occasional clump of bushes or "bluff" of young poplar, and here and there a tall spruce. To the north, a range of hills marked the Onion Lake Reserves, and twelve miles to the east could be seen the high rounded cone of Frenchman's Butte.

But nothing stirred on the opposite bank or on the trail that led across the uplands. They drove down the steeply twisting way to the water's edge, and cautiously forded the first channel to the sand-bar. The men began to work at once, loading the clumsy boat, rowing it back and forth across the deep channel until all their goods were piled high on the north bank, where Elizabeth prepared the noon meal.

There was plenty of time while the men worked, and she decided to make bannock, to try the quick skill she had learned from her husband's sisters. On the trail, there were still those who could mix it deftly in the mouth of an open sack of flour, but a basin was safer for a novice. Flour, salt, some fat, then just enough water—it was all in the quick light touch, she had been told—and the soft press of her palms would take the place of a rolling-pin,

45

shaping the bannock to the heavy iron frying-pan, pricking it with a fork. She would make enough for a day's supply for themselves, and for Peter Taylor too. She was immensely pleased when the men pronounced it good, as good as any they had eaten on the trail.

Hour after hour passed, John Grace climbing to the highest point, pacing irritably, swinging back and forth along the trail. Elizabeth rested in the shade, noting how the shadows slowly moved, changing as on a sundial. When they heard the sound of wheels, it was late afternoon; and they watched incredulously as the Taylors drove towards them.

This was not the strong team and wagon they had expected, but another buckboard, old and flimsy, with wheels that wobbled uncertainly and made a squealing protest with each turn; and it was drawn by one poor horse, a thin sway-backed colt of no more than two years, tired from the twelve-mile drive along a hot and dusty trail.

John Grace hurried towards them. Elizabeth heard his voice, sharp with anger. "What's this? Where's the wagon you were to bring?" And Mr. Taylor was stammering an explanation. They had stored all their belongings in one room at the Mission, and he would come again for them. They had so little luggage with them that there had been no need to hire a wagon after all.

"No need!" Matheson's voice was harsh, choked with anger. He stood for a moment before he went on abruptly, waving his hand towards the farther bank. "Well, there's a wagon over there, and a buckboard—with good teams. The man's waiting for you. I'll get what we need for tonight." He walked rapidly down the winding trail to the level where their goods were piled.

The Taylors climbed down from their rig, and stood in a huddled group, whispering together. Elizabeth, waiting stiff and silent, a little apart from them, could only marvel that people could be so helpless, so unable to carry out their part of an agreement. She felt more pity than anger. John Grace's was enough. But she could not move, could not think of anything that she might say.

Mrs. Taylor turned, smiling uncertainly. "I'm so very sorry, Mrs. Matheson," she said, still whispering. "We—we didn't realize. We thought an Indian would surely come this way with a wagon." The timid voice impelled Elizabeth to speak more loudly than was necessary. They could work it out some way—manage somehow.

She suggested that the Taylors should unload their things—carry them down to the boat. They responded almost with thankfulness to the suggestion, began piling their luggage hurriedly at the side of the road—"Before John Grace gets back," Elizabeth thought.

46

Mr. Taylor came towards her, fumbling in his pocket. He held a key out to her. "To the room where we've stored our belongings." Elizabeth regarded him in silence, and he went on hurriedly, "I'm sure I can trust you." Amusement twitched her lips. "Oh, I'm sure you can, Mr. Taylor." She took the key and slipped it into her pocket.

John Grace came over the last rise in the trail, with their bags and "grub-box." He put them into the back of the buckboard and nodded to Elizabeth to take her place. She shook hands hurriedly with Mr. and Mrs. Taylor, spoke to the children, and moved towards her husband. "You must speak to them," she whispered. "They meant no harm." He helped her into the rig, and then walked back to where the Taylors waited. "A pleasant trip to you." He spoke courteously, but still unsmiling, and shook hands. "Peter will help, if you take the boat across."

Elizabeth waited for him to take the driver's seat. Instead he handed her the lines, walked to the colt's head and tugged at the bridle. "Get moving," he snapped, "or do I have to put you into the back and pull the whole thing myself?" There was no humour in his voice. As the colt moved forward, he dropped his hold on the bridle, but went ahead, the buckboard following him slowly.

Elizabeth turned to wave to the Taylors, still waiting by the side of the road. "They haven't much to carry," John Grace answered without turning. "They'll manage. If they can't, what are they doing in this country?" And walked steadily on. She flicked the lines on the colt's back to hurry it along. It seemed that all the brightness had gone from the day.

They went in silence for an hour that seemed endless to her; then where the trail curved close to a lake, he stepped aside until she was level with him. "As good a place as any for supper," and he smiled. "Could do with a bit of that bannock under my belt for the miles ahead."

His anger had passed. When they drove along the trail again, he walked beside her, whistling now and then, and finally breaking into snatches of song—old Scottish airs that she remembered Janet had sung at Burnbrae; and tunes that were unfamiliar to her, the rollicking songs of French boatmen and their sons, the buffalo-hunters of the plains.

At a poplar "bluff" where wild roses bloomed in profusion, he stopped again, and cut several branches, stripping them of thorns as he carried them to where she waited in the buckboard. He laid them in her arms. "Oh, my luve's like a red, red rose."

It was then that they saw the Indian, a young man on horseback, who had drawn aside from the trail to watch them pass. John Grace called to him in Cree, and he came towards them at a lope. The two men talked in the slow deep speech that had no meaning for Elizabeth, until her husband remembered and told her, ''This is Sam Cook. He'll get a wagon and bring our things to us tonight.'' They shook hands, and the young man turned his horse and was gone from sight in a swift gallop.

John Grace was measuring each mile, recognizing landmarks as they made their slow progress. She wouldn't see the lake, just off the road, that gave its name to the place. The Indians called it We-cha-ka-skoo-se-ya Sa-ka-ye-kun, the lake of the bad-smelling weed—but the wild onions that grew there had been known to early travellers, and added a change of flavour in hot rubaboo or ruchow, though pemmican of itself was good enough. He could do with some of it again.

There, in the distance, dark against the sky—a tall spruce. It marked a camping place with a good spring of fresh water. Cart brigades had halted there a good half day's journey from Fort Pitt. This rich pasture land was where the Hudson's Bay Company had kept their horse guard, as many as three hundred horses to spell off those that had come all the way from Fort Carlton or Fort Edmonton.

She would see the settlement soon, just north of the old camping place, closer to the hills. There had been no settlement when he had come this way last, though the two Missions had had their start before 1885. There had been a farm instructor for the Reserves—George Mann—and now he was the Indian Agent. They had moved the Agency to Onion Lake from Frog Lake, with its lonely graves of the nine men who had died in the massacre of 1885.

The buckboard moved down towards a creek, the colt quickening its pace. When it stopped to drink, John Grace swung to the seat beside Elizabeth, and as they moved up the other slope from the creek, the settlement came suddenly into sight. ''We're home,'' she cried and heard his voice speaking the words with her. They laughed spontaneously as children, linking fingers for the wish that would follow.

The long day had reached that moment when the very air seemed golden with the light of the low sun, before the first trailing brush strokes of colour flamed into the wonder of sunset. As they approached the Mission, John Grace pointed to an old man sitting at the door of a small log building. ''John Hope—one of the first Indian boys trained at Red River, seventy years ago. He's been Taylor's interpreter. He'll be moving on, to Thunderchild's Reserve soon. I'll speak to him and see about the horse. Must be his. I'll meet you at the house.''

The house stood waiting, silent and empty, sunset reflecting from its windows. Like a child's drawing—two rooms up and two rooms down, a door here, a window there. Elizabeth walked around it to the front door, and entered a bare room. Beyond that was the kitchen, ashes spilling from its stove. The air, heavy with the day's heat, held the scent of wild strawberries, and she found a bowl of them on a rough table by the window—a gift from shy Mrs. Taylor.

The rooms echoed to her steps. There would be another empty one above, and a locked door to the furniture in the second. She would rather be outside, she thought, and carried the bowl of strawberries with her to the step outside the lean-to porch. She waited there, tasting the warm crushed fruit that stained her fingers, sitting with her back to the wall, the roses wilting beside her.

The wooded ravines of the hills were slipping into shadow. She caught the flash of a scarlet tunic from the log barracks on a low hilltop; heard the sound of men's voices and their laughter as they called to one another in the stillness of the evening; identified the Agency buildings and the frame dwellings of its employees in a line at the foot of the hills. The Roman Catholic Mission was a little farther west, along the same trail by which they had driven; and in the hills just north of that Mission, the Hudson's Bay Company post had been built.

High above her head, a night-hawk swooped with a sharp zing, and a bat flickered from under the roof of the little frame church across the yard. As her husband came to where she waited, he followed her glance, but with a builder's eye. "Have to buttress that. Must be a foot out of plumb, but it'll have to wait. It's this house'll need all the work I can give it first. Hope tells me the Taylors huddled in their coats around the stove most of the winter. Structure's sound enough, but every door and window needs reframing."

She walked with him around the house as he appraised it. He stopped briefly to wave towards a scraggly patch of ground. "Our garden. One head of cabbage, Hope says. No use planting anything, Taylor thought, when the fence was broken anyway, and they would be leaving. Hope has fifty hills of potatoes behind his house. Can spare us a few."

As they entered the house, he turned to consider the porch. "First thing tomorrow, I'll move that stove out here. Give us an extra room." He stopped at the foot of the stairs. "Been up?" Elizabeth shook her head. They walked together to the empty room above, and then stopped at the locked door of the second. He tested the handle, a look of disbelief on his face. Then he turned sharply to her.

"All right, Bessie, hand over the key Taylor gave you at the river." The disbelief was on her face now. "You couldn't have seen that." "Did I have to? To know that there was something in the wind? You don't really believe, Bessie, that even with your help, Taylor's any match for this old hand at cards and horse-trading? Over with it."

She handed him the key. "He said that he was sure he could trust *me*." "And so he can—to see that I don't break in. This is our door and our house now." He swung the door open, and they looked into a room crowded with furniture and boxes. John Grace stripped the blankets from the bed, and closed the door again. "These'll do. We can sleep on the floor in the other room."

The room was bright with moonlight when she wakened to the sound of a wagon pulling in under the window, and her husband's voice speaking in Cree to Sam Cook—and then interpreting. "He'll sleep under his wagon till daylight, and give me a hand with the lifting."

She fell asleep again, knowing quite well at what hour daylight would come and the work begin, and that she was as eager as he to be at it.

Nine

The charge of St. Barnabas Anglican Mission at Onion Lake included those two Reserves of Sekaskooch and Makaoo, and stretched north and west to Island Lake (Ministikwan), Frog Lake, Little Fishery and Moose Creek.

The Indians to the north were Bush Cree, living as hunters and trappers, as all the Cree had been when fur-trading began, and the acquisition of guns in the eighteenth century had made it possible to compete on the plains where the Blackfoot were dominant. Earlier, the Blackfoot had come into possession of horses from the Spaniards to the south, and as their skill developed in the buffalo chase, their range extended as far north as the Saskatchewan River, and west to Fort Carlton. With guns, the Cree could venture from the bush to raid Blackfoot encampments and steal horses, becoming in their turn equally skilled riders, and dependent as the Blackfoot were upon the vast buffalo herds. In the warfare that ensued, these Plains Cree drove the Blackfoot west to the mountains, and during the late nineteenth century were themselves the dominant tribe on the prairies.

They were a fierce proud people, contemptuous often of their meeker brothers who remained Bush Cree. But then the buffalo vanished; and with starvation as the only alternative, the Plains Cree had had no choice but to make treaty with the Canadian Government and be limited to Reserves.

Big Bear had been their undisputed leader in the last resistance to Treaty Number Six. He was a remarkable man, fully aware of the inevitability of change, yet hopeful that he could mould his proud people into one force, capable of exacting better terms from the government, without resorting to the folly of warfare against overwhelming strength. Even when he finally signed the Treaty, late in 1881, he refused to choose a small Reserve that would isolate him, and brought his Band of about five hundred intransigent Plains Cree back from the Cypress Hills to the Saskatchewan where he had been born. From Fort Pitt, they had moved on to Frog Lake in the winter of 1884, where Riel's envoys constantly stirred their unrest. Finally, with the news of Gabriel Dumont's success in the encounter at Duck Lake, Big Bear's control of his fierce young warriors was defied, and he had to remain the helpless witness of massacre.

Onion Lake was on the trail between Frog Lake and Fort Pitt, and the Indians had come that way after the massacre. At Frog Lake they had killed the Roman Catholic missionary from Onion Lake with his brother priest. But one of their converts, Toussaint Calling-Bull, ran the twenty-five miles to Onion Lake, not daring to risk the sound of horses' hooves, to warn the two white men who remained there, the farm instructor, George Mann, and the Anglican missionary, the Rev. Charles Quinney. They escaped with their families to Fort Pitt, but were taken prisoners there by the Indians, with Chief Trader McLean, his family and others, when Big Bear negotiated the surrender of the fort. The detachment of North-West Mounted Police, stationed at Fort Pitt, were then permitted to leave on scows down the river to Battleford. The Indians withdrew with their prisoners a few miles down the Saskatchewan to Frenchman's Butte after Fort Pitt was partially destroyed.

It had been built in 1829 and was an important Hudson's Bay Company post in the days of the buffalo hunts; but those days had passed, and with them the fort's importance. Nor was its location on the river of any consequence after the Saskatchewan had ceased to be a main artery of the fur-trade. From 1872 until 1883, Factor William McKay was the officer in charge, and he was succeeded by two of his sons, Angus and Junior Chief Trader William McKay.

They were the fourth generation of McKays who had served the Hudson's Bay Company, two of eight sons, all of them educated at St. John's College in Winnipeg, James to become a Judge in Saskatchewan, George an Archdeacon of the Anglican Diocese in Saskatchewan, and the others to continue in the service of the Company.

After the Rebellion, the younger William McKay returned to Fort Pitt, partially restored it, and then moved the post in 1890 to the hills at Onion Lake, nearer the northern Indians who continued as trappers.

The McKays were not the only ones in the settlement at Onion Lake who had had a long association with the Hudson's Bay Company. James Simpson lived there too, after his retirement from the service. He was a son of the famous Governor, Sir George Simpson—one of seventy sons, Elizabeth was told, and every one given at least the opportunity of an education and suitable employment with the Company. Historians would not support such a record, naming only five sons, one of them James Simpson.

Benjamin and Louis Patenaude were his stepsons. In 1839, a large party of Metis buffalo-hunters had come from Red River to make Fort Pitt their base, tracing the first overland route from Fort Garry—the Carlton trail that wound westward past Fort Pitt to Fort Edmonton. Isidore Dumont had been their captain. His son, Gabriel Dumont, was then only three years old, and he settled later at Batoche; but descendants of the other hunters remained near Fort Pitt and Onion Lake. Their names sound a roll-call of the earliest voyageurs and boatmen of the fur-trading companies: Dumont, Nolin, Dufresne and Patenaude, Mellon, Trottier, Parenteau, Salois, Fortier, Amirault, Cardinal, and Laframboise.

Their allegiance was to the Roman Catholic Mission at Onion Lake, and through them there was a close link with the Indians, though only a few of these were as yet converts. A house-chapel served the Mission in 1884, and the first church was built in 1888. Three years later, four Sisters of the Order of the Assumption came to establish, first a day-school, and then a boarding-school.

With the Metis as congregation, and a trained and dedicated group of workers, their school from the start was larger and possibly more effective than the Anglican one. In fact, when the Mathesons came, the work of the Anglican Mission had scarcely begun. True, it had had its nominal start in 1879 from Fort Pitt, when the Rev. Charles Quinney was appointed missionary by the first Bishop of Saskatchewan, the Right Reverend John McLean. But there were few converts on the Reserve, and though one family took the surname of the first missionary, their head, Manito-nikik Nakaykisis, had been converted, not by the Mission, but as a prisoner at Stoney Mountain Penitentiary with other Plains Cree after the Rebellion.

Two chaplains had been appointed to counsel the prisoners, both of them men of human understanding, and of rare ability. Samuel Pritchard Matheson was the one assigned by the Anglican Church, soon after his ordination in 1876. By 1885, he was also deputy headmaster of St. John's College, and Canon of the Cathedral; but, like most who had grown up at Red River, he knew Indians and spoke some Cree. These prisoners responded to his ministration and nine asked to be baptized in the Christian faith. All of them requested the name of Samuel Matheson, and he had to explain the confusion that that could bring, suggesting instead the names of the apostles, Manito-nikik taking the name Thomas, with the surname Quinney.

The Roman Catholic chaplain had been specially assigned to the work at that time because of his long friendship with the Indians. He was the noted Oblate, Father Lacombe, who had been sent to the Fort Edmonton district in 1852, and had served for ten years at Lac Ste. Anne and St. Albert before he was given "the mission of coursing the prairies to try to reach the poor savage Crees and Blackfeet." He had won their respect by his undoubted courage and dedication, and in 1885 the Blackfoot Indians responded to his counsel when they resisted Riel's incitement to rebellion.

In the winter of 1869-70, during his years as missionary free-lance, he had journeyed up by dog-sled to Rocky Mountain House. "As chance had it," he would recall, "Jack Matheson, a young trader from the Red River, was going up to the Mountain House, and he proved an interesting travelling-companion. For this lusty young giant . . . was brimming over with gay spirits, with lore of the hunter's world and tales of the early settlement at the Red River. Matheson himself was to come in time, through many wanderings and a life of much colour, to be an Indian missionary in the Church of England. But on that trip, behind dogs to Mountain House, there was little thought of prayer or preaching in the rollicking young trader's head."

In the years that followed that trip to Rocky Mountain House, the irresistible old missionary diplomat was to travel as far as Europe, and back and forth across Canada; but he had not forgotten Matheson, and when he came to the Roman Catholic Mission at Onion Lake in the late summer of 1892, he walked down the road to visit him.

The place seemed home-like then, though the simple furniture was improvised largely from packing-cases. Still, there were two rocking-chairs in the sitting-room; and Elizabeth had unpacked the treasures she had bought in bazaars a world away, the room glowing with the draped colour of a red and gold sari, bright lacquer, and shining brasses. While the men talked, she served them tea; and the old priest, rocking gently, sighed "Ah, Matteson, Matteson—you are too com-for-table; you will lose your sal-va-tion."

The evident friendship between the two men, their easy companionship, made Elizabeth aware of how little meaning there was for either of them in the prejudice that from childhood she had accepted as valid. She remembered how, in the school at Burnbrae, where there had been one Anglican family, she and the other little Presbyterian girls would draw their skirts aside whenever they passed in the playground, hissing "Papist". She had learned to chant:

53

Piscy, Piscy, bow and bend,
Sit ye doon and rise again.

and knew the response that could come:

Presby, Presby, never bend.
Sit ye doon on man's chief end.

She had had practically no contact with Roman Catholics, in the Orange-tinged communities of Ontario particularly, but in Manitoba too, and had thought them truly beyond the pale. She marvelled when the Sisters made their own call on her at the Mission, not long after Father Lacombe's visit. The Sister Superior noticed dark rings under Elizabeth's eyes, inquired as to her health, and then prescribed the standard remedy of that day, usually at hand, a dose of castor oil.

It would be many years before Elizabeth could come to John Grace's easy acceptance of them all as varying individuals, no more extraordinary than any others. The difference in his attitude was part of his Red River heritage, where active boys ranged far in a diverse community; but it was also definitely formed and strengthened during his early years in the Territory of the Saskatchewan.

At Lac Ste. Anne, he had been accepted as one of John Cunningham's family; and Cunningham's wife was a Metis woman, a simple and most devout adherent to her people's faith, whose ardent longing was that one of her sons might become a priest, and who strove to influence John Grace to the same calling. She had failed in that one particular; but now Father Lacombe told Matheson that her son, Edward Cunningham, had served his novitiate, and might be sent to the Mission at Onion Lake. When he came, he had not forgotten his boyhood admiration of John Grace; and to their vague connection the two men applied the term "cousin". That was Red River custom. They used the Cree more often—calling one another "Ni-chi-wam", my brother.

To the Indians, competition between the two Missions was quite incom-prehensible. "The white men offer us two forms of their religion; but we in our Indian lands had our own. Why is that not accepted too? It is the worship of one God, and it was the strength of our people for generations."

Matheson had his own experience with Indian resistance when he tra-velled from Onion Lake to visit the Band at Island Lake, thirty-five miles

54

up into the bush, by a pack-trail that went uphill and down, "crooked as a snake track", past lake and muskeg. He found the camp deserted except for a few old men and women, who would tell him nothing. He knew Bad Hand, their Chief, only by name; and he made another effort, travelling in a horse-drawn toboggan, by the only slightly easier winter trail—with the same result. The implication of that deserted camp was clear. They wanted nothing of him and his teachings.

Then Edward Matheson came to Onion Lake, with the Rev. D.D. McDonald of Thunderchild's Reserve. A rider appeared, asking all three missionaries to come to Island Lake. They reached the encampment and were led to the Chief's teepee. Edward Matheson and McDonald were admitted, but a young Indian at the entrance dropped the flap then and said in Cree to John Matheson: "You do not enter." In sharp surprise, he snapped, "Why may I not enter?" He spoke in Cree too, and the young man laughed. "So you speak our language?" And lifting the flap, said simply, "Tawao —there is room."

The men within were silent as Matheson took his place in the circle about the Chief. Then Bad Hand broke the silence. "I shall tell first of days that are past, when we roamed as free men. A band of Cree made their encampment at Red River, and one day a boy rode out from the white Settlement. He was red-headed and his horse was poor, raw-boned. Some of the young men raced about him on their swift ponies, yelling at him in Cree. He gave no answer. It was as if he could not understand. Then one of them whirled a lasso, and shouted, 'Let us take him back to the camp. The women can make dye from his hair for their work.' And at once the white boy snatched his lasso, whirled it, and shouted back in Cree, 'Two can play at that game.' The young men raced back then to their camp, and the old people said, 'We told you Cree is a big language.'"

The Chief waited. Matheson's face was as impassive as the Indian's, but his hand went up to touch a white plume in his greying hair. "Are not my words true?" Bad Hand asked. "They are true," John Grace replied. "Once I was a red-headed boy, and I rode a raw-boned horse."

"And I was the young man who swung his lasso first," Bad Hand said simply, and paused before resuming. "The years passed. And then the government in Ottawa sent a man who knew all about plants, to explore the southern plains. He had a red-headed guide. The two of them camped in the Eagle Hills. Women came from a Cree encampment, asking for tea. The guide could not understand them, it seemed. A woman showed him a handful of tea-leaves that had no more strength, from many boilings. And he seemed to understand then. He emptied the used leaves from his tea-pail and offered those. The women left with angry words, but he smiled as though he had given them what he thought they wanted.

"The next day, the man who knew about plants came to talk to the Indians, and the guide was with him to interpret; but when he tried to enter the tent, a man stood in his way, and said 'You do not go in.' His words were Cree. The guide said quickly, in the same tongue, 'Why do I not go in?' The other laughed, and held back the flap at the door. 'So, you speak our language. Tawao.' "

Bad Hand stopped for a moment. "Are my words not true?" he asked again, addressing John Matheson directly. "They are true. The man who knew all about plants was John Macoun. In the summer of 1879, I was the red-headed man who supplied his transport. I met his party at Fort Ellice, with horses for the iron-bound carts they brought by river steamer from Fort Garry. We travelled all through that summer, west by north first, along the Fort Carlton trail, and then westward, passing Last Mountain Lake.

"There was plenty of water; and poplar bluffs for wood. The flowers everywhere excited Macoun. This was the country that Palliser had called desert. When we passed the head of Long Lake, the men saw the level empty sweep of the plains for the first time. I taught them how to use buffalo chips for fuel, that the horses liked slough water, and that we could carry enough good water for ourselves.

"When we came to the Elbow of the South Saskatchewan, Macoun set his surveyors to measuring the height of land between it and the Qu'Appelle. The government hoped to build a canal, so that they could use water-stretches instead of a continuous railway. The surveyors found a difference of eighty-seven feet in a distance of eleven miles, and that scheme ended.

"While they measured, I made a boat to carry all the equipment with the carts and buckboards across a river half a mile wide. It took us two days to get everything across. We took a course then for the Hand Hills, but Macoun sent the others ahead, and he and I started north-west to Battleford, 125 miles, for the rest of the supplies. He had his compass always, but I still used my wits. We took only enough food for ourselves, and when we came to the Eagle Hills, we were boiling our tea until the leaves had no more strength. The women who came to our camp would not have believed me. I had my fun teasing them, pretending that I did not understand, even when they called me bad names."

The answering flicker of a smile touched Bad Hand's face, and he said, "I was the man who stopped you at the door of the tent. Now, we meet again, and you are a missionary for the white man's religion. I have my own, and the Great Spirit himself has told me that I must keep it. I have strong spirit power, and have been a conjurer, one of the secret society of medicine-men, Mitawiwin. I will not turn to your belief, but you may come to teach my people whenever you will.''

Ten

Throughout the long days of that happy summer of 1892, Elizabeth and John Grace worked together, the sound of hammer and saw to be the continuing accompaniment to life at St. Barnabas Mission. Of all the activity that filled Elizabeth's days, it was the work that she shared with her husband that meant most to her. Only rarely could she accompany him on his visits about the Reserves since they lacked any conveyance of their own, and he either walked or drove with others. In his building, however, he did need an apprentice, and to his satisfaction and her own happiness, Elizabeth proved an apt one. Carpentry would never lose its appeal for her.

Teaching was supposedly his job—the school a log building two miles nearer the centre of the Reserve. He went daily, but only six or seven children were registered. Attendance was not compulsory, and might vary from two or three to none at all. He considered it a waste of his time, and

Onion Lake residents at the Indian Agency (1901).
Back row: Sergeant Hall, John Matheson, Charles Garson (H.B.C.), William Sibbald. Elizabeth is standing in front of John Matheson—Annie Phillips is at extreme right. Mrs. Slater is standing at extreme left, next to Mrs. John Hall.

welcomed the Rev. Isaac Taylor when he returned to claim his furniture. It seemed that he was still waiting for the Bishop to assign him to another Mission, and thought he might try to learn Cree. The aimless, casual work of the school would give him something to do during the weeks he remained at Onion Lake.

With undisguised relief, John Grace turned to work more satisfying to him. The Indian Agency operated a lumber mill on the creek that came down a ravine in the hills; and he selected what he needed to make the necessary repairs to the house and to enlarge the porch into a proper kitchen, twenty by twenty-four feet, that could serve many purposes. Then he buttressed the church strongly, and partitioned it to make a classroom at one end, so that Elizabeth would be able to undertake the teaching duties for which she was much better qualified than he.

In the meantime, she was well occupied too. The simple layette for her expected child had been finished with fine needle-work; and for the baby's shawl, she had unpacked one of softest camel's hair that she had brought from India. It had been intended for her own use, but would serve this truer need until it became quite thread-bare.

She was buoyant with health and energy, not in the least worried as her time approached. She had asked a white woman to attend her, the only other one except for the Sisters. It was a natural enough inclination, and John Grace said nothing to alarm her. The woman was capable—when she was sober. She was much more likely to be drunk, however, if given the least excuse—and that was supplied by an Indian woman who came to the Mission on the morning that Elizabeth's labour pains began, and who carried the news promptly. When her help was sought, the intended midwife was quite incapable of giving any.

Matheson turned at once to run the mile to the Hudson's Bay Company post, most of the distance uphill. He appealed to Mrs. McKay, and then raced back again on foot to the Mission, while she waited for a horse to be harnessed. At four in the afternoon, the child was born, a healthy ten-pound girl. They named her Gladys Elizabeth, but to her father she was always N'tanis (my daughter) or simply Tannie.

That same afternoon one of the Mounted Police rode down from the barracks to visit John Matheson. Years later, he told Gladys how the two of them had talked together, and how Elizabeth had served them tea with quiet composure. Before the visit had ended, however, Mrs. McKay called John Grace from the room, and he excused himself, returning in a few minutes to tell the astonished man: "I have a child, a fine daughter."

She was a lovely baby, and her fairness enchanted the Indian women, who came daily to see her. One of them brought Elizabeth a moss-bag that she had made, of black velveteen, skilfully beaded, and embroidered with bright colours.

It found immediate use, though without the dried sphagnum moss that gave it the name, and that the women gathered in the northern muskegs and carefully dried for their own babies' use. Elizabeth's baby was clothed as any other white child of that period, in flannels and long petticoats, and then laced into a bag.

It seemed to her mother a wise precaution, for the women who visited the Mission were used to handling infants laced firmly into these bags; and they could not resist this child. One in particular would spend hours with Gladys, claiming her as her own. She was herself one of twins, a rare birth to the Indians; she and her sister had been named Dayblanket and Nightblanket. They had been the wives of one man, and after his death Nightblanket had become the wife of Sawhao, a brother of Jimmy Crookedneck, one of the finest Indians on the Reserve. When he died, she was simply "Sawhao's Widow", and feared as a medicine-woman because of her vindictive nature. Her sister was quite different in temperament, and for her own skill was called Dancer. No one was afraid of her and there was probably no reason to be concerned for a baby in her tender care. But the moss-bag offered security, and, having adopted it, Elizabeth was to continue its use for all her babies, certain of each child's welfare with any voluntary nurse, and of the comfort and warmth it provided when a winter trip was necessary.

When Gladys was six weeks old, Elizabeth began to teach in the improvised classroom in the church. She made a small deep hammock for the baby, and swung it in the school or in the kitchen, wherever her work was. Meanwhile she was learning to speak Cree. The child was a natural link between her mother and the Indian women, and language seemed no longer a barrier, for it was easy in such friendship to practise the words and phrases that they taught her. In addition, John Grace had arranged for regular lessons with one of the older sons of the Quinney family, and Joe was a faithful and lively teacher.

The beautiful autumn days of that year lengthened into weeks, without any snow until November 19. Matheson was able to complete the repairs and building he had planned; and there was time as well to prepare the fields and gardens for spring planting, for it was his intention to make the Mission as self-sufficient as possible. At least one horse and cow would be a first requirement, and chickens and pigs; and so there must be a field of oats, and possibly wheat; and the potato-patch would need to be large, and the vegetable garden; and both properly fenced with rails.

Planning was all very well, but in the meantime they had to manage as best they could, buying what they needed from the Hudson's Bay Company post, stocked for the Indian trade, and from the Indians themselves. Under the direction of the Agent, George Mann, the Band had a fine herd of cattle, chiefly for beef. The Mission was given one cow, but she was a wild range animal quite impossible to milk for all their experienced effort. Instead, she provided beef for that winter, and a glossy coal-black rug for the floor; while William Vivier, on his way each morning to the Roman Catholic school, brought them a five-pound lard-pail full of milk.

Yet with what seemed to be barely enough to bring themselves through that winter, they still followed the plan they had been considering. The day-school had proved quite ineffective, the attendance haphazard. They were certain that the only course that could succeed with these half-wild children would be to take some into the Mission house to live, and there teach them English and reading and writing, but particularly the practical skills essential to their changed way of life.

Other missionaries had reached the same conclusion; and Elizabeth, on her part, had been impressed by the remarkable work of a Mission of Faith in northern India. This project of theirs would have to be another act of faith, for the Church could not be expected to finance the venture. Indeed their plan was in effect before Bishop Pinkham learned about it and gave his approval, though it would be another two or three years before he was able to raise John Matheson's annual salary to its maximum of $600. It was a grant from the government that paid the initial salary of $300 to a recognized school-teacher on an Indian Reserve; and there were rations of 1 lb. of beef, 1 lb. of flour and 4 oz. of biscuits per day for each child in attendance —nothing on Sundays and rations only for children who were Treaty Indians, a ruling strictly enforced.

Just after the first snowfall in November, early in the afternoon of a fine clear day, John and Elizabeth Matheson began their tour of the Reserves at Onion Lake. They drove in a borrowed jumper, a home-made, one-seated sled, drawn by a single horse. They hoped that they might persuade a few families to accept their plan, and they visited every home that was not definitely Roman Catholic, and where there were children of school-age.

They could count fifty or more such children; and John Grace used all the persuasion possible, arguing and cajoling in Cree—but to no avail. No one would part with a child—until they came to the house where Martha Painter had found a corner for herself and her small daughter, Minnie. The mother was almost blind, a poor, unwanted, ill-used woman, who fended for herself in the summertime and, when winter came, crowded into any house that would give her a corner. Yet it was not Martha, but the others in the house who pushed the little girl forward when John Matheson made his appeal for children.

Minnie was five years old, and wore only a long cotton dress and moccasins. She came with Elizabeth reluctantly, half-frightened, almost sullen—until a turn in the road hid the house from sight. Then John Grace said something to her in Cree, and smiled. To Elizabeth, the words seemed nothing but magic, for Minnie's small face flashed into a *gamine* grin, her eyes sparkled, and she burst into a torrent of laughing Cree, revealing herself suddenly as a bright, responsive child. She had accepted them, and the Mission was to become the only home she would clearly remember.

She was alone with them for only a few weeks, for their tour of the Reserves had its effect as soon as the Indians could gather for long councils together. Four big boys came to the Mission of their own accord, a few children were brought from other Reserves, and the first child who was not a Treaty Indian was accepted. Before the winter ended, there were ten or twelve children at the Mission. Bunks were built at one end of the kitchen for the boys, and the girls had a double row of them in the larger room upstairs, which Mr. Taylor had finally vacated, taking his furniture with him.

The clothing that the children wore was seldom adequate, and sometimes had to be burned. Elizabeth made capotes and trousers for the boys from grey blankets; and then George Mann sent more blankets and heavy cloth from the Agency store-room. He provided some rough lumber as well for the building they had to do, and the government rations of beef and flour. The Indians began to bring frozen fish, game and wild meat; and for these Matheson gave trade in kind. Now and then he went hunting himself, returning after one mild moonlit winter's night with one hundred rabbits, which an Indian woman skinned, taking the pelts as her share.

When spring came, there was a rush of work in garden and field, sometimes with hired horses and labour, more often with the help of the boys and girls, as part of their training.

Spring also brought that wild longing for freedom from all restriction; and one or another of the boys and girls might disappear suddenly, to be found again in some camp. Minnie proved one of the most irrepressible, escaping time and again to the freedom even of her mother's poor tent. Elizabeth made her a dress of bright red that delighted the little girl, and the absence of its flash about the house or grounds was clear indication that John Grace would have to track her, and reclaim a child entirely willing to return with him each time.

One day, however, she was not at her mother's camp, and Martha admitted that she had taken her to the Roman Catholic Mission. It was not surprising to find the poor woman ready to play one Mission against the other, in hope of some larger bonus in gifts, but Matheson insisted that she come with him to see the priest.

They met, their conversation all in English, for the priest was new, and had no idea that the Protestant missionary spoke Cree. Any other he had known might read the prayers in halting Cree, but needed an interpreter for the simplest speech. He agreed with Matheson that to take Minnie into the care of the Sisters had been a mistake that he should correct. And then, while John Grace listened with impassive poker-face, he heard the priest tell Martha, in his own imperfect Cree, that it had indeed been a mistake—in so far as the Protestant was a big man, and evidently somewhat angered. But she could bring Minnie again, and they would make certain that steps were taken that would prevent another withdrawal.

Martha was puzzled. John Grace said, in English, that perhaps it would be as well if he explained it to her himself. In his easy fluent Cree, he told her that Minnie had been registered at the Protestant Mission, and could not be withdrawn when there was no reason, for she was happy there and well cared for. He would take her back with him, and there she would stay.

He left with Minnie, and the silenced priest watched as they walked down the trail together, the little girl holding to the tall man's hand, skipping to keep up with his long strides, but laughing as she ran, and chattering gaily in Cree.

And when he talked of the incident to Elizabeth, she remembered a visit from Sister St. Patrick, and the whisper as she left, "Why did you do it? Why did you take them into your home? Now, we shall have to do the same."

Eleven

Summer advanced into autumn and brought its own concern to Elizabeth. She had conceived a second time, and then developed severe mastitis, her breast becoming swollen and inflamed. No remedy that she could apply to the suppurating abscess had any effect, and she knew that she must make the long trip to Battleford to see a doctor, taking Gladys with her, and leaving John Grace with temporary help at the Mission.

Edward Matheson had left Battleford to return to his former charge at Prince Albert, and it was arranged that Elizabeth should stay with Mrs. Campbell, the mother of a young policeman who had been stationed at Onion Lake.

The mail-stage from Battleford reached Onion Lake every third week, and Sam Ballendine was the driver. This time he had agreed to return a horse and buggy to its owner in Battleford, and Elizabeth could drive that. The little girl was just learning to walk, and could be strapped in the seat beside her. It would be more comfortable and convenient for both in the separate rig; and Ballendine would be watchful and considerate in his own driving, taking responsibility for the horse at each stopping-place.

It was a three-day trip, for Ballendine slowed his horses whenever he noticed that Elizabeth had had to stop hers; and on the last day, held them almost to a walk. Late in the evening, they came to Battleford, lamps lit in many of the scattered houses. Ballendine took her directly to Mrs. Campbell's house, and jumped from his own rig to lift the sleeping child from the buggy, and help Elizabeth dismount. She had reached the last of her strength and could barely lift her arm. She trembled with weakness and pain. Mrs. Campbell had opened the door at the sound of the wheels, and waited in the light that streamed from it. Elizabeth tried to thank Ballendine again, but he stood twisting his battered hat in rough hands, embarrassed, mumbling that it was nothing, nothing at all, that anyone would have done the same for her.

Donald Campbell had carried the child to a couch, and when he turned to Elizabeth, his voice was disturbed. He would go at once for a doctor, he told her, but it wouldn't be any use. There was a banquet that night at the Queen's Hotel—it had started hours earlier, and there wouldn't be a man sober, certainly neither one of the doctors. Still he would try. But when he returned it was only to say that a doctor would come to see her in the morning. In her numbed condition, it seemed to Elizabeth that a few more hours could make little difference; she might be able to rest; the abscess might even burst of its own accord.

The doctor who came in the morning was the Police surgeon, haggard evidence of the night's celebrations. He gave her only a cursory examination, and muttering "Badly swollen", turned to his instrument bag. She waited for further examination, but when he turned, his hand concealed a scalpel taken from his bag. "You'll feel better now," he said, and as she looked up at him, his hand stabbed the scalpel into the throbbingly painful breast. Blood and pus spurted the length of the small room. Elizabeth fainted.

When she regained consciousness, the doctor had gone. Mrs. Campbell was dressing the wound, and half-crying as she worked. Whether the tears were in pity, or in vexation for the state of her room, Elizabeth did not ask. The little girl began to wail aloud, and her mother spoke to her instead, stretching out a hand in comfort.

It was two weeks before she was strong enough to travel that long road home. This time she had an almost royal escort, a detachment of North-West Mounted Police, all scarlet and gold, two men in a democrat, two riding. They travelled fast.

She was driving herself again, with the child strapped to the seat beside her; and the horse she drove had grown old in the Police service. No longer eager for the trail, he would respond to her whip with only a short burst of speed, and then fall back again into his own easy jog-trot.

All day long she had to urge him on constantly, to keep within sight of the Police. Now and then, one of the riders would gallop back to make certain that all was well with her. But the trail was a long and lonely one, deeply rutted, intersected by other trails that wound in equal loneliness across empty country, or simply offered a better way around some impassable mudhole of the spring. They might drive all day and not see another human being.

That is why one simple incident fixed itself in her mind, recurring in the wakeful dark like a nightmare whenever the memory of that trip returned to her. She had been whipping the horse to bring him within range of her escort, when her hat blew off, the wind turning it over and over back along the trail they had just come. She pulled the horse to an abrupt stop, and jumped from the buggy. It was only a minute or two before she caught the hat and ran back to her seat beside Gladys. The horse was cropping the grass at the edge of the trail, and she whipped him again in pursuit of the riders.

There was nothing more to it than that; and yet late that night she wakened, gripped by the fear that would return always to haunt her. It seemed to her that the horse had not dropped his head to graze, that something had frightened him, and he had left the trail, the buggy crashing behind him as he galloped across open country; and she was crying for her baby, and running, running, running forever across an endless empty prairie. She must have called out, for she wakened, and one of the men spoke. "Just a bad dream," she answered, and put her arm around the sleeping warmth of her child to feel that reassurance and return to sleep herself.

They had camped that night in the haying shack of one of the Bresaylor settlers, used only seasonally. It was of rough logs, its floor of hard-packed earth, its roof of sods across poles, its only furniture the stove. The Police hung blankets from the poles to screen a corner for Elizabeth and the child, and laid her bedding roll there. In the morning, in the first light of day, she heard the men's low voices, and the crackling of fire in the stove. A hand pushed a basin of steaming water under her curtain. "You might like some hot water for yourself and the little girl."

She would not distinguish his voice from the others, nor remember them by name, but she would recall that little extra courtesy added to their kindness in the preparation of meals, the care of the horse, the consideration that lifted her above a duty imposed upon them. Yet when they reached the north bank of the river and the familiar road from Fort Pitt, she could be relieved that her dependence was ended. The old horse could amble if he chose, and she could rest her whip arm. She waved it cheerfully at her escort, the child waving too, as the young men disappeared in a last flash of colour round a wooded turn of the trail.

Back at the Mission, she was well and strong again, her pregnancy as happy as the first had been. The child would not be born until March, and she resumed her duties with full vigour.

The enrolment in the school would remain fairly constant at ten or twelve for the first years, but only six could be registered as Treaty Indians. One of these was under-age when he was accepted, and so barred from any grant. He was taken for the same compassionate reason as Minnie, and was to remain until he was eighteen.

The other pupils, as "non-Treaty", were quite outside the responsibility of the Department of Indian Affairs. Matheson wrote directly to the Department on behalf of those who were children of Indian mothers—"orphans or deserted by their fathers, in most cases illegitimate, waifs and outcasts among the Indians, with no one to care for them." The reply was not unexpected. "It would appear to be a bad policy on the part of the Indian Department to put a premium on illegitimacy."

Non-Treaty children were usually from outside the Reserves, and Matheson came to know of them as he resumed—almost without intention—his old role as trader, finding in that skill, means to support the work adequately.

By the winter of 1893-94, word of the school and its acceptance policy was being carried from one trapper's family to another, in the area north of the Saskatchewan River. Ten years earlier, the government had established Industrial Schools, but these were for Treaty Indians only. Now, Indians who remained outside Treaty, and fathers who were white men or of mixed race, and whose children had little or no chance of schooling, learned that

65

non-Treaty children were accepted in Matheson's school at Onion Lake.

These men had known of him for years, and some had been early friends and associates of his. A few came at once, others more slowly over the years, from Saddle Lake and Long Lake, from Beaver River and from Cumberland House; and there were some who had settled in the Battleford district, or who came from Fort Saskatchewan, from Medicine Hat, from Red Deer. Their families often accompanied them to the Mission, and a few of the children were white, though usually there was some Indian blood. The parents had one request to make—that the opportunity offered in training and in elementary education might be their children's too.

While it was as a trader that John Matheson came to know these families, it was his skill as a builder that was even more apparent at the Mission. Convinced that the school would grow, he added one whole wing to the Mission House, so that there was room for at least thirty children. Meanwhile the church had to be restored to its original purpose, to accommodate the Indians who came each Sunday to visit their children and to listen to a missionary who could speak to them in their own language, and in terms they understood.

To serve once more as a school, the log building was brought from its former site near the centre of the Reserve to the Mission grounds, and Elizabeth continued her instruction of classes there. "An accomplished teacher," Major McGibbon was to report when he made his inspection of the Protestant schools; and he went on to note: "The pupils are doing very well . . . the usual industries, knitting, sewing and housework for the girls, who also make aprons for themselves and shirts for the boys. The boys do gardening, tanning hides, a little carpentrying, cutting wood and attending to stable."

That stable held as yet only a quiet old mare and one cow, each to have a remembered and honoured place in the history of the Mission. Maud had been Edward Matheson's well-fed, easy-going mare. She had suited him admirably and when he left for Prince Albert he had parted with her reluctantly, though with the generosity characteristic of both brothers. Elizabeth and John Grace remembered the more spirited horses they themselves had owned, but were thankful for Maud and would recall her with affection when her service ended with dramatic suddenness.

The cow was a Durham that gave two pailfuls of milk morning and evening, and had to be milked at noon as well, though she gave only a pailful then. Her progeny in the years ahead were to be the strong nucleus of a herd that outgrew the Mission pastures, and such a remarkable cow deserved a remarkable name. They named her for Alwilda Lake, whose husband had been the telegrapher at Fort Pitt. The station was moved to Onion Lake, but he was transferred to another, and had willingly sold his amazing cow to the Mathesons.

Mrs. Lake came to the Mission for a visit before she left the area. She was welcomed by Elizabeth, happy to have another woman with her in the last week before her confinement, to help in the child's delivery. That Mrs. Lake was evidently alarmed at the prospect made no impression. The woman had a child of her own, and surely some experience. But when Elizabeth's hour came, that nervousness gave way to utter panic. Alwilda fled the house.

It was too late for John Grace to go himself for help. The McKays had left Onion Lake, but he was certain that Mrs. Benjamin Patenaude would come, and he sent one of the boys racing to the stable to harness old Maud. At that moment he heard Elizabeth's voice in frightened alarm, and he called to the boy, "Don't spare the horse," and ran back to the room.

An old Indian woman had thrust herself in, eager to assist; but Elizabeth had learned that it was usually their custom to cut the cord too close, and then stop the bleeding with a paste of astringent herbs that they kept with them for such purpose. She was terrified for her baby, and her Cree was quite inadequate to make the old woman understand. John Grace settled the matter simply by putting her out of the room, and delivering the baby himself.

Meanwhile, the boy had taken his order quite literally not to spare the horse. Maud was galloped along a snow-filled road to Patenaude's farm in the hills, and then back again with Mrs. Patenaude, only to drop dead at the stable door.

The child was another girl, so fair in colouring that the Indians named her Whitehead. John Grace wanted to name her Caroline Emma for two friends from earlier years who had been helpful in support of the work at the Mission. Neither name appealed to Elizabeth. "Carrie? Emma?" She tried the sound. "Just those last syllables," John Grace suggested. "Rie-ma". And baptized with the full names, she was never called by either, but only Riema, or Rie.

The delight that Gladys found in her baby sister was refreshing. Their mother's attention was scarcely divided anyway, for it still had to be given to all the others too, in the work of the household and the school. Gladys was a venturesome child in any case. One day that summer she escaped the Mission and wandered down the trail until her small legs wearied and she fell asleep in the tall grass at the edge. Ka-nē-pu-tā-tāo (He moves as though with many legs) happened to ride that way. He had been one of Big Bear's headmen, the chief dancer. When his horse shied suddenly and he saw the child, he lifted her to his beaded saddle and brought her to the Mission. Everyone was searching for her when he gave her to her father, telling him with amusement that his own small son could wander farther than Gladys had, and still find his way back to camp. When he had reached manhood, he might make his way to the Mission, to claim the girl his father had found.

Her baby talk was all in Cree, encouraged by the other children and by the women. They had been holding her the day she took her first steps on small beaded moccasins, whispering gently to her, encouraging her until she ran to Elizabeth laughing "Ni-ka-wiy", (my mother).

Now she would offer the same encouragement to this baby, crooning the soft language, until Riema in her turn could respond—two small tow-headed children, speaking Cree—Gladys all quick impulse, Riema gentle and soft, but ready to follow her sister in any venture.

They had another companion then, a little girl to whom Cree was truly her mother tongue, and whose black hair and dark eyes accented the Mathesons' fairness. She was just two days older than Riema, and had been born in a camp near the Mission. Her mother was Rosalie; her father a casual white man, utterly disinterested that a child had been born. Rosalie, like other women, could fend for herself; and Rosalie did. Elizabeth, in much gentler care, was startled to learn that the Indian mother was out snaring rabbits before her baby was a day old.

Yet the child flourished. Rosalie chose for her the name "Maria", though the letter "r" is unknown in Cree and was quite impossible for her to sound. On her tongue, it became "n", and she added the Cree diminutive to the name as well, "Little Maria" becoming in her mother's soft voice "Man-ia-s". Manias was scarcely a year old when her mother conceived another equally casual child to another white man. Elizabeth's horrified "How can you do this, Rosalie?" brought a reply that humbled her. "You are a white woman—not poor and helpless as we are to any man." Rosalie's tuberculous cough even then had doomed her, yet she bore that child too, another daughter, and clung to her with pathetic love; but she was unable to look after Manias any longer, and brought her at two years of age to the Mission where her two older brothers had already been placed in the care of the Mathesons.

Twelve

When the spring of 1894 came, John Matheson's trading had produced gratifying bales of fine furs, chosen with a discerning eye for quality, as he made certain that any tentative venture into that field would confirm from the start his reputation as a trader.

He took the furs to Battleford that year, and when he returned he was reasonably satisfied with what he had accomplished in trade, but convinced that Battleford and the high cost of freighting supplies from Saskatoon could not serve his purpose.

Edmonton was a much more logical trading centre for the north Saskatchewan territory. The railway had been extended from Calgary, and wholesales and warehouses were developing. It was no farther a trip by wagon from Onion Lake than to Saskatoon, and he could make the return journey on scows down the Saskatchewan—a faster, easier way of travelling, the most economical means of transporting heavy goods, and as familiar to him as the old cart brigades along the Carlton trail had been.

That renewing of old acquaintance with the trail and river would have to wait for another year; and in the meantime the Mission engaged his whole attention. Bishop Pinkham had made his visitations and was well satisfied with the progress of the work, and with the studies that Matheson had followed. It was arranged that they would meet again at Duck Lake for John Matheson's ordination as deacon.

The work of the Mission was becoming known even beyond the wide episcopate of Calgary-Saskatchewan. At Holy Trinity Church in Winnipeg, the Rev. C. C. Owens had made a stirring appeal in its support; and in eastern Canada, the Woman's Auxiliary to the Missionary Society had undertaken, as their first venture in that regard, to pay the salary of a worker at St. Barnabas Mission. They had a volunteer from Holy Trinity congregation, Annie Eliza Phillips, who could begin her work early in 1895.

She was in her early twenties, and had come to Canada as a member of the staff at Government House in Winnipeg. Her intensive training in household service had begun in England when she was little more than a child, under an uncle who was a butler; and her ability and evangelical fervour had won high praise from Lady Schultz.

John Matheson was not impressed by the recommendation, nor by her own glowing references to Sir John and his lady; yet both he and Elizabeth found the young woman a most engaging and intelligent person, eager to undertake any duties. Her ability lay particularly in training the girls in household work, though Elizabeth did have to impress upon her that at the Mission the strictest economy had to be practised, and only the simplest fare provided.

As soon as the fields and gardens were planted in the spring of 1895, John Grace left for Edmonton with his bales of fur and bags of seneca root, then in demand for pharmaceutical purposes as an expectorant.

He took with him some young men, two of whom would drive the horses and wagons back to Onion Lake, while the others worked as capable axemen, building scows of heavy timber, under his direction, on the banks of the river at Edmonton.

There he was well remembered; and, in the light of his earlier exploits, there was less comment on his appearance as a trader and riverman, than on his activities as a missionary. To old acquaintances, it was the latter that often brought surprise.

On the way down the river with his scows, he stopped at Fort Saskatchewan, and at the noon hour was hurrying up the hill to the North-West Mounted Police barracks, past the Superintendent's house, when Mrs. Griesbach saw him. "Matheson!" she shouted from her doorway. "By the

Colin Fraser's scows at Athabasca Landing (1911). This shows how John Matheson would assemble his own scows at Edmonton between 1895-1912.

living lights—John Grace! Haven't seen you in years. Come on in for dinner. What're you doing now?''

"Working for the Master," he called back.

"Fine," the Superintendent's jovial lady roared, "bring him along too."

Elizabeth had known from her first acquaintance with John Grace how readily his person and his activities captured the imagination of others. Now, from the telegraph station on the hill at Onion Lake, Jack McFeeters sent down news items from Edmonton about Matheson and the progress of his work. The Dominion Telegraph line in the North-West was not twenty years old, and operators still considered it almost a private domain, relaying gossip to one another, even playing long-distance checker games to pass the time.

McFeeter's successor, Herbert McCleneghan, may have been one of the last of such telegraphers. During the Rebellion he had been one of the operators at General Middleton's headquarters at Fort Qu'Appelle; and then had served the Dominion Telegraph at Battleford, Duck Lake and Bresaylor before coming to Onion Lake. He was practically blind, and to him the reality of the world lay in those clicking keys. The office was simply a room in their house, and his wife and family learned to transcribe with ease the code that was their second language, a living means of communication with the world outside.

With such relayed news items of John Grace's progress at Edmonton, Elizabeth was prepared when a telegram came from him personally, advising her that the scows had reached Moose Creek and would unload at the landing nine miles from the Mission.

Word went out at once through the Reserve, and every cart, every wagon, every conveyance that could hold together was on the trail to the river. Elizabeth stayed in charge at the Mission, which hummed with excitement. It would have been impossible to hold the children to the usual routine. They were on the trail too, racing after the wagons and carts for a ride, sharing food at the campfires at the river, often trudging most of the way home again behind the loads.

At the Mission, Elizabeth checked each conveyance as it pulled into the yard, watched the unloading, directed the placing of barrels and boxes, and finally helped to estimate the payment due each freighter. Camps sprang up across the road; women and children came with their men to trade or simply to visit; and after dark, the sound of drums, the rhythmic chanting of the dance encompassed the Mission, until in the magic of the summer night, it seemed to drift into another world, back into an undefined and ageless way of life.

The profitable journey and safe return had a stimulating effect upon both John Grace and Elizabeth; but while she found her satisfaction in the completion of the trip and his return to the Mission, his fulfilment lay in the enterprise itself, in its challenge, and in the release from the day to day routine of the Mission. In Edmonton, he had renewed old friendships and old skills during crowded days that had been given to trading and to building the scows and loading them properly. Each day had been marked by some achievement, but the challenge reached its peak when the scows were poled out into the surge of the river at high water, to begin their run down the Saskatchewan.

He would make that run year after year, usually with two, sometimes with four loaded scows; and never was the journey quite the same, except for his constant vigilance. Sometimes the scows had to be moored at the bank each night; sometimes, with high water and fine weather together, a great sweep would be fastened to each scow to keep it in mid-current, and it would glide down-river all night, a man on guard.

John Grace could exult then in making the three hundred twisting miles in less than two days, running the rapids, catching the drift of the current skilfully. He would seem all vigorous energy, for this was the life he loved—to match his skill and experience, and the young strength of his men, against the power of the mighty river, to know its rapids and its shifting sand-bars; and often to drift smoothly through tranquil summer days, with their ever-new, ever incredible wonder of bird-song and scented bloom; the towering banks of the river opening before him, with scarcely a sign of human habitation, and no sound but the deep voices of his men, the uprush of sudden wings, the stirrings of wild life in the solitude.

When routine had been restored at the Mission, he turned to building more adequate storehouses, training some of the older boys and the young men he often employed. Time had to be given to book-keeping too, as he reduced the Edmonton accounts and all the pencilled notes on scraps of paper to a careful list of estimated expenditures and receipts, in preparation for his report to the Bishop, with a brief financial statement.

This balanced exactly, as each subsequent one would, but only because of two items listed under receipts—one of these his entire salary, which only rarely in any of these statements would appear again as an expenditure—the other that final comment "contributed from private sources".

"This work is simply a work of faith," the Bishop would note—and marvel, "faith abundantly rewarded. Additions have been made to the

buildings, the institution is well equipped throughout, and there is no debt!''
An exclamation mark escaped, to be followed by the puzzled comment,
"How so much can be done with so little visible means is simply wonderful."

Neither John Grace nor Elizabeth could have supplied an answer to that,
so complete and unhesitating was their involvement in that "work of faith".
Even in looking back upon that time, many years later, Elizabeth could add
only her own query, "But given our training, and that evident need, what
else could we have done?" In 1895 she experienced the full meaning of that
commitment.

Thirteen

Elizabeth had felt no regret for her abandoned studies in Medicine. The
inadequacy of any available medical attention concerned her, but no more
than it did anyone else.

Tuberculosis was common, and not confined to Indian Reserves, though
its spread was practically unchecked there. Its treatment seemed to be still
uncertain; death was almost inevitable. Elizabeth had grieved when Ben
Quinney's beautiful young wife died, for Mary and she had become close
friends. They had made it a practice of meeting early each Sunday morning,
to go to the Cree service together, arms about one another. But Mary had
died within the year, and in friendship Elizabeth had been able to do as much
as any doctor might have done.

But when she recalled two other deaths on the Reserve, she knew that such
reasoning could not apply. A young woman had died of general peritonitis
from a retained placenta, having had only old mid-wives to attend her during
a difficult delivery; an old man had died of septic throat when a fishbone that
he had swallowed could not be dislodged. Either death might have been
prevented could the doctor have come quickly, and been sober.

Ay-im-i-hōs (He who knows misfortune) was a living accuser; and it was
against her that he had levelled the charge of cowardice when she had
refused to amputate his foot. It had been badly frozen and gangrene had
developed.

At the sight of it, Elizabeth had cried in dismay, "I would not dare to
amputate." And she had appealed to John Grace. "Explain to him that I
cannot do it, that he must go to Battleford, or get Mr. Mann to send for the
doctor." But Ay-im-i-hōs replied angrily in Cree, and turned away in scorn.

"He says you are a coward," John Grace translated reluctantly. "He will not wait for a doctor to come. He will not go to Battleford. If he must die, it will be here amongst his own people.''

And the next day, she learned that Ay-im-i-hōs had amputated his own foot, with his son's help, using his hunting knife and a common saw.

''Why did he think I could do it?'' she had asked; and John Grace reminded her that it was of her own doing when she had inspected the herbs that Sawhao's Widow used and from her knowledge of botany had warned of their effects. How had she known? Was she a medicine-woman too? And she had laughed, telling them of her brief venture into that field. She had only started, she told them.

But Ay-im-i-hōs, in his desperation, had not accepted that. Here was someone who should be able to help him. And he came to her even a second time, when gangrene appeared in the mutilated stump. She found herself compelled to say once more, ''I would not dare to amputate.'' He would have to go to a doctor. But Ay-im-i-hōs was his own surgeon again, with the success that his stoic courage merited.

Any regret for her interrupted studies that these incidents brought was lost again in her happiness and satisfaction in the work at the Mission. She had made her promise when she said that she would marry John Grace. She would forget her studies in Medicine, and be happy simply being his wife. And she knew that in their work together, and in their little girls, their love had grown.

That the success of their venture had required another worker, she could almost regret, though it was still with amusement that she sensed Annie Phillip's devotion to John Grace and her anxiety to please him always. Any competition there was quite unequal, as it was in the younger woman's growing self-assurance in her duties. Elizabeth could meet both on her own grounds, aware of her own capability, and much more certain of the constancy of John Grace's love.

She was quite unprepared when she realized that he had resolved to send her away to resume her studies; and she would never forget the shock.

He had asked her to go for a walk with him, up into the hills, escaping the interruptions of the Mission, leaving Miss Phillips to her duties. They walked quickly, and he went without speaking, as though impelled by some urgency to reach the top of the long hill. Elizabeth was breathless when they came to the great triangular stone near its crest. He stopped, and she went up the inclined slope to sit on the edge against which he was leaning, looking down, through the wooded ravines towards the Mission.

He filled his pipe slowly, pressing the tobacco with his thumb. ''What do you think of Miss Phillips?'' he asked abruptly, and she had laughed with amusement. He repeated the question, adding, "How is she managing the work?''

"You know that as well as I do," she retorted. "She's quick. Her training is helpful. She's ready to learn. After all, she's young.''

"Not much younger than you are.''

"Five or six years. She's well-trained, and the boys and girls seem to get along with her.''

"That's not what I'm asking," he repeated. "Can she manage the work?''

"She does what she's asked to do, and she does it well. But what do you mean by 'manage'? That's still my job in the house and the school.''

"Then I'll answer the question myself.'' He stopped to examine his pipe as though it were not drawing properly. "Have to say it straight out. She can manage the work. With Miss Phillips here, you can go back to Medical College.''

"Go back?'' Her cry echoed from the ravine. "Go back? But I don't want to go back. Have you forgotten so soon? When I promised to marry you, I said that I would give up that old dream entirely, that all I wanted was to be your wife. This is my whole world now—the Mission, you, and the children. Do you really think that I still want to take up studies I left seven years ago? You are my life, you and our children, and our work together.''

When he spoke again his voice was gentle, but with a note of firm reasoning that he might have used with a child; and like a child she drew her feet up onto the stone where she sat, tightening her arms around her knees to still the trembling. "It isn't because I don't believe that, but four years ago I was thinking of myself, of my need for you. That hasn't changed, but other things have—our work, our responsibility for all these children in the Mission. We should have a doctor here. Battleford is too far away. You've known that yourself, time and time again during these years.''

"What if I have? Does that mean that I'm the one to be that doctor?''

"And who else is there? Unless I send Miss Phillips to Medical College.''

"Miss Phillips! Miss Phillips!'' The pain that tensed her gave way to unrestrained anger. "Must I hear nothing else? First, it's Miss Phillips who can so easily do work that I've trained for all these years, teaching, at Marchmont Home, in India, and here, learning step by step how we can enlarge the work and improve it. But she can do it easily now, she can 'manage' with no more preparation than household service. And now it's she who can go in my place to Medical College. Why, she stopped school before she was twelve years old. Don't you realize that it will be difficult enough for me to make up what I've lost in these seven years? What do you think it takes to pass those examinations?''

He gripped her shoulder, but she jerked away. "What does it take?" His voice rose in anger too. "What does it take? It takes what you have." He controlled himself with an effort. "Let's not shout at one another. You know I'm right in what I'm asking of you. You've known it ever since Ay-im-i-hōs came for your help, and you couldn't give it."

"You never will forget Ay-im-i-hōs."

"Neither will you."

"But he could have gone to Battleford."

"And die in a strange place. That's what it meant to him. I visited him in his camp. It's hard for him to get around, but the stump has healed completely. He showed it to me, and asked me 'When will your wife learn to do work like that, and not be afraid?' I told him, 'Now. I'm sending her back to College.' ''

Elizabeth sat quite still. "Then it's decided that I will go," she was thinking. "This is the total commitment of a man, and it includes his wife and children."

She lowered herself from the stone, shivering suddenly; and he put his coat around her shoulders. There was comfort in the gesture, but the chill that she felt was in her heart, not in the air. Far below them, the evening bell of the Roman Catholic Mission tolled.

"We'll have to hurry," was all she could say.

During the few weeks that remained of summer, Elizabeth drove herself through long hours, thinking that under the pressure of work she could escape the unhappiness that pressed upon her. Sewing offered some release, and it was beyond Annie Phillips's capability. Clothing had to be prepared for the winter, made over and adjusted to size. Much of this clothing now came in missionary bales from the east, but there was new material too from which further clothes were fashioned; and there was always mending to be done.

She would turn from sewing to gardening, or to that work in the kitchen that would always give her satisfaction: the preserving of fruit that the Indian women brought in birchbark rogans.

None of the work, however, could quite overcome the discouragement she felt and the lingering resentment that she should be expected to separate herself from everything that had grown most dear to her and submit herself to the discipline of hard study. Only gradually was this tempered by her own resolve that she would accomplish what was expected of her, that she would carry out her part in this further commitment, at any cost to herself.

When she knew that she was pregnant again, and that the child would be born before the spring examinations, she said nothing to John Grace until it was too late to withdraw, determined that she would use the time she had in College to review and advance her studies, and that to postpone her return for another year would only make everything more difficult.

In September, Annie Phillips was left in charge at the Mission while John Grace drove Elizabeth and the two little girls to take the train from Saskatoon. They stopped in Battleford. It had become once more, for them all, a refreshment of family bonds, for Edward Matheson and his wife had returned from Prince Albert.

There had been a change that year in the government's policy for Indian Industrial Schools, and Edward Matheson had assumed charge at Battleford. In the several Industrial Schools that had been established in 1883, costs had ranged from $138 per pupil to more than $230 while the government carried full financial responsibility. Now it had been decided that these schools should be operated on a strict per capita basis, at an average of about $130 per pupil, with some allowance in addition for capital expenditure. Under this plan, the Anglican Church had direct control of the Battleford School.

It was recognized that it would have to be operated much more economi-

Battleford Industrial School, 1883-1914. It also served as the Government building for the North-West Territories when Battleford was the capital, 1877-1882.

cally than under its previous head, for the cost per pupil then had been more than fifty dollars higher than the grant presently allowed. Undoubtedly the efficient operation of the much smaller boarding school at Onion Lake influenced Bishop Pinkham and Archdeacon Mackay when they asked John Matheson's brother to accept the appointment as principal. Their choice was fully justified, for Edward proved most capable. With a staff of twelve, and an enrolment of about one hundred and twenty pupils, the School continued under his careful administration until 1914, he and his brother working in close cooperation all through those years, to the advantage of both schools.

The per capita plan set for Industrial Schools had been applied to Emmanuel College in Prince Albert, which had become a school where Indian boys were trained as teachers. Now the grant was extended to the Mission boarding school at Onion Lake, though at the much lower level of about $70, paid only for those pupils who were Treaty Indians. This undoubtedly helped in the financing of the school, but the policy of accepting any child remained unchanged.

In the large principal's residence at the Industrial School, the family from Onion Lake was welcomed. If there was the least strain, it was understandable, for Elizabeth came with two lively little girls—Ray Matheson had lost both her babies, the first a still-born son, the second a daughter who survived only briefly.

As they continued the long drive to Saskatoon, Elizabeth realized that her reluctance to return to study had diminished, that she was looking forward to it with some of her former enthusiasm and interest. That very fact made her more conscious of how hard their parting was for John Grace. She was going to something challenging and new, and her children would not be too far from her; he was returning to the loneliness of work that she had shared closely with him, separated from her and his children.

There were tears that neither of them could quite restrain, and seeing these, Riema began to wail. Gladys put her arms comfortingly about the child. "Don't you cry, Ne-se-me-sis, my little sister. You'll break your mother's heart."

They spoke to one another in Cree; and in Winnipeg this proved so amusing to others that they retreated at first into shy silence. Then their usual friendliness prevailed, but it was in hesitant English that they spoke.

It had been decided that the little girls should stay at Poplar Point with their Aunt Christiana; Elizabeth would stay in Winnipeg with her husband's younger sister, Eliza Lamb. Eliza's nature was as lively and out-going in friendship as her brother's; but Christiana's life had imposed its own unhappy restraint, tempered for the little girls by the presence of others, and particularly their gentle grandmother.

Elizabeth registered at the Medical College, which was more than a mile from her sister-in-law's home, and she walked across open prairie to the lectures, in all kinds of weather.

She was the only woman attending that year, though two others had graduated from the College. She was accepted readily, receiving credit for her entire first year at Kingston, and for the two second-year classes that she had completed in the summer of 1888. This meant that her course was not too heavy, and that she had time to review and strengthen all her work.

At Christmas she wrote and passed the term examinations. She then went to see Dr. J. R. Jones, the lecturer in obstetrics, who was acting Dean. When she said that she would be withdrawing, he surprised her by trying to dissuade her. She was a good student, he told her. Had anyone made the year difficult for her as a woman? He knew that that had been the experience of women in other Colleges. His concern amused her, and she laughed. ''I wasn't expecting to have to tell you, Dr. Jones, that I am seven months pregnant.''

''Who is your doctor?'' he asked. She hesitated for a moment before admitting that she had none, but she gave no explanation. ''I'll take the case,'' he said. She remembered that she had heard, ''Whoever wants J. R. Jones, pays for J. R. Jones,'' and he noticed her confusion. ''There'll be no fee, of course,'' he said, and then added, ''After all, it is rather unusual to be able to attend one of my students in childbirth. Send me word when you need me, and I'll come at once.''

And when she did send word, he came; and then decided that he would go on to make some other calls in that neighbourhood. ''In that case, Doctor,'' she told him, ''I can only say that it was kind of you to come, but there will be no need to come back. I'm certain of that.''

''Your judgment against mine. I'll wait half an hour.''

Twenty minutes later she called to him. He was talking to her sister-in-law in the next room, and jumped a low stove that barred his way, snatching a clean towel from the washstand to wrap about his hand and arm, for there was no time to scrub before the vigorous child was born, another girl, more than eleven pounds in weight.

She named the child Letitia, for John Grace's mother; and took her to stay with her sisters and her grandmother at Poplar Point until the spring break-up was over and travelling easier.

Synod was meeting early in June at Prince Albert, and John Grace had planned to meet them there; but when she arrived with the three little girls, it was Edward who met them instead, and arranged for transportation on the river steamer *The North-West,* making one of her last runs up the Saskatchewan to Edmonton. John Grace met them on the third morning as the steamer moved upstream from its night's anchorage at Pine Island, some ten miles from Fort Pitt.

Fourteen

Elizabeth turned readily again to her summer's work at the Mission, and the weeks went swiftly. There had been no wavering in her resolve to complete her studies, and to return to College that September. But it was with some reluctance that she thought of returning to Manitoba, for she missed the companionship that she had known in Kingston with other women.

The College in Kingston had closed in 1894. She had written to Toronto and knew that the Ontario Medical College for Women would give her credit for all the work she had done. She would have to complete some second-year classes, but she would be allowed to register as a third-year student. She lacked matriculation Latin, however, and would be required to write that before she could continue into her final year.

The year presented a formidable challenge, yet she felt ready to accept it, for the months in Winnipeg had restored both her confidence and her interest. It was for other reasons that Toronto could be impossible for her—the extra expense for travel, and arrangements for the care of her six-month-old child. It seemed that she would have to return to Winnipeg with her baby, relying upon the kindly hospitality of John Grace's sister.

Gladys and Riema could stay at the Mission with their father. Early that year, Edward Matheson had sent one of the senior girls in the Industrial School to be Annie Phillips's assistant. Matilda Black was only eighteen, but a happy-natured, capable girl, who adapted readily to the Mission. "I call this school my home," she wrote to her former school-mates. "We are just like one family."

In late August, John Grace drove Elizabeth and the baby to Saskatoon. They camped on the river-bank, and he went to a house to ask if he might have water from their well. Mrs. Stewart was a stranger to him, but she asked if she might come back with him to the camp and meet his wife. The baby drew her attention. What would Elizabeth do with the child while she was at Medical College? Then, suddenly, with the child in her arms she said, "Would you let me keep her? Mine are grown, and the days are often lonely. I'd take good care of her. Anyone will tell you that."

The warmth of her appeal seemed the answer to Elizabeth's perplexity when Mrs. Stewart agreed to accept payment for the child's care in that pleasing foster home. Yet she would remember the wistful longing in the woman's eyes as she held the baby.

When she reached Winnipeg, Elizabeth was experiencing some distress from the abrupt weaning of her child and was fearful that mastitis was developing. She had not yet registered at the Medical College when a message came from W. R. Mulock's office asking her to call. He had been acting as her husband's lawyer in certain business transactions, and she expected that that was the reason. Instead Mr. Mulock asked about her medical studies. He and his wife had both shown a kindly interest during her previous year, and believed that she would be happier in the Ontario Medical College for Women in Toronto. Would she accept a forty-dollar cheque from them to pay the additional travelling expenses? Call it their missionary donation, since they believed they could put this money to no better purpose. Elizabeth accepted with gratitude, and that night left for Toronto.

During the long train journey, her discomfort increased. Once more there was that throbbing pain in her breast, and fever. In Toronto, she called at Dr. G. Gibb Wishart's office. He was the secretary for the Ontario Medical College for Women, and she registered first and then asked for his medical advice. It was quite definite. She was not to go on with the work. She was simply not fit to undertake it. She tried to explain that she had to. "If you knew my husband, you would understand. The work we are doing means everything to him, and I cannot fail him. I don't think I could forgive myself, nor could I return to him a failure."

Without her knowledge, Dr. Wishart wrote to John Matheson, urging him to recall her, advising him that she was not well enough to undertake such work. He was answered with a telegram, referring him to Luke 9:62: "No man, having put his hand to the plough, and looking back, is fit for the kingdom of God."

This was a woman's hand to the plough. But Dr. Wishart's hand was there too, for she had found a strong ally. His treatment had arrested mastitis; and in the interval between letter and telegram she had proved her resilient strength and was well again, ready to go on. Among young students once more, she remembered her eager associates at Queen's; but now she was a woman in deep earnest, for whom the months of study held one overriding purpose—to complete the undertaking

81

that would restore her to her husband and her children at the Mission.

She worked steadily and hard, though she continued that strict observance of the Sabbath that had been part of her training from earliest childhood. There could be no study on that day. Instead she found her way to the Sackville Street Mission, and worked as a volunteer there. It served as relaxation, and proved to be a satisfying and happy association with others. One of these, Caroline Shaw, offered to go to Onion Lake to help in Elizabeth's place, and left Toronto in the early spring.

Elizabeth completed her second-year work before Christmas, her third-year work in the spring of 1897, and was successful in the examinations. Then she concentrated on matriculation Latin, her tutor a scholarly old clergyman, and she passed that examination too, in June.

She was ready to return to Saskatoon to claim her child. John Grace, however, could not meet her there, for he had to wait at Battleford for the arrival of the Bishop of Athabasca, who was to ordain him priest.

That was the year of Queen Victoria's Diamond Jubilee, and Bishop Pinkham was attending the Archbishop of Canterbury's Lambeth Conference in London. Bishop Young had agreed to make the visitation of missions in Saskatchewan Diocese, in the vigorous manner that was characteristic of him. Accompanied only by his wife and son, he was travelling down the Saskatchewan River from Edmonton to Prince Albert, in a sixteen-foot canoe.

The exact time of his arrival at Battleford could not be certain, only that his stay would have to be brief; and John Matheson came from Onion Lake to await him there, arriving at the Industrial School on the thirtieth of June. On Sunday morning, July 4th, the Bishop's canoe swept in to the landing, and the ordination service was conducted that afternoon at the school.

Elizabeth arrived in Battleford on Monday, both train and stage having been delayed. Those days on the trail had been most difficult for her. She had come to Saskatoon eager to claim her little girl, and had found herself resisted as a stranger. It was a painful experience for both mother and child, and one that Elizabeth was actually no more prepared to understand than the child was.

The trouble began as soon as she called at Mrs. Stewart's after her train had reached Saskatoon. She was met with a certain wariness, as though her coming had been dreaded. It was early evening, but the child was asleep. She was asked not to waken her, not to take her away to a strange bed in a strange house; and she could only agree to the sensible request. The stage, however, would be leaving Saskatoon at seven in the morning, and she

82

reminded Mrs. Stewart of that before she went back to the stopping-house, disquieted and lonely.

Very early in the morning, when she called again, the child was toddling about the house, still in her night-dress. Mrs. Stewart made no effort to interest her in her mother, nor to encourage any friendliness. Instead she made the direct request that Elizabeth should not take her away, should let her stay for another year at least, until her mother's course at Medical College was completed. It did not surprise Elizabeth, after the experience of the previous evening. She wondered if Mrs. Stewart had not been building on that hope from the very start. Elizabeth, to her, was an unnatural mother, who could not possibly love her children and be willing to leave them to become a doctor.

There was no time to try to explain, nor did there seem to be any possibility that the child would be returned willingly. The two women faced one another, one pleading for postponement, the other firmly resolved to act, while the child watched uneasily, sensing the tension.

Then Mrs. Stewart tried a last resort. It would be impossible to take Letitia that day. All her clothes were in the wash. She pointed to the tub outside the door, on a platform that ran along the side of the house. Elizabeth walked to it, rolling up her sleeves. The tub had been hastily filled with cold water, and the clothes were clean, some of them still in neat folds. She wrung each garment, and tied them all together in a tight bundle. Then she asked for the child's blanket, and Mrs. Stewart gave it to her in desolate silence, and stood watching as Elizabeth wrapped it firmly about Letitia and lifted her in her arms.

She turned once again to Mrs. Stewart, but there was nothing that she could say to ease the pain of parting, and she walked away, one arm firm about the protesting, struggling child, the other carrying the bundle of wet clothes that she would have to dry as they travelled.

The stage was waiting for them. Elizabeth set the child on the high seat of the democrat, and climbed up beside her. Letitia was quite silent now, a small withdrawn person, making no response to the friendliness of the driver, nor to her mother's efforts to interest her. Nothing in Elizabeth's experience or studies could have indicated to her that a child, to whom no harshness or unkindness had been intended, could still suffer shock in this second disruption of all that was familiar to her.

When they made their stops along the trail, Letitia would not walk, but only crept; and Elizabeth, knowing nothing of such regression, was vexed with a stubborn child. "She has turned against me," was all that she could think. "Will it be the same with the others? Have I lost them too?" And when they came to the Industrial School, she gave Letitia willingly into the care of an Indian girl, and then noted with slight jealousy how the child responded to the girl's warm laughing acceptance of a baby. After the first small hesitance, Letitia also responded warmly to John Grace, and he was certain that Elizabeth was being simply too impatient with the little girl.

School holidays had started and Battleford was quiet again after the celebrations of Queen Victoria's Diamond Jubilee on June 22, 1897. The opening ceremony had been at the Police Barracks, where cannons fired the royal salute, and Major Cotton addressed the schoolchildren. In the afternoon, there had been sports and horse-racing on the Battle River flats, dinner at the picnic grounds, and a dance at the Barracks in the evening, all for the admission ticket of 50¢ for an adult and 25¢ for a child.

Some twelve hundred Indians had encamped on the flats at the mouth of the Battle, and had been granted permission for a Sun Dance, which was followed with feasting when the Agent distributed beef, flour, bacon, tea and tobacco. The campers were returning to their own Reserves when John Matheson came from Onion Lake with Jimmie and Mary Crookedneck, two of his finest people.

Jimmie had not been well during the trip, and he was dying when the doctor came to the camp on the flats. That he was dying of typhoid fever caused no particular alarm. Typhoid was simply another of the maladies usual in any medical practice of the day.

To John Matheson, Jimmie's death and Mary's grief were of deep concern. When the funeral was over, more than the usual number of mourners gathered at the widow's camp, and in leaving each took a gift. It was all according to custom, but on this occasion Mary was remote from the protection of her own people, and everything that she possessed was taken before John Matheson heard about it.

Angry with the unfeeling mourners, angrier with himself that he had not foreseen this possibility, he hurried down from the School to where Mary sat by the ashes of her campfire, her face hidden in her long hair, loosened and disarrayed as a sign of mourning. The anger that he felt swept through the whole encampment. Within an hour, Mary's possessions had been restored to her.

She returned with the Mathesons to Onion Lake. The trip took only two days for they travelled in a light democrat, behind a team of fast horses. When they camped at Twin Lakes, Elizabeth was amazed to find how quickly and neatly Mary could make camp. In these skills, she found some release from her grief, and helped Elizabeth at a time when Letitia's continued resistance to her mother presented its own problems.

Once they were back at the Mission, the difficulty with Letitia seemed to resolve itself, at least on the surface, much more easily than Elizabeth had dared to hope. The other little girls were waiting there, and they had forgotten neither their mother nor their baby sister, encouraged as they had been to remember them and finally to count the days and hours to their return. The greeting was warmly demonstrative, and Letitia had little choice but to be drawn into the circle over which Gladys held sway as the eldest, and which now numbered five small girls—for Rosalie had given to the Mathesons her sixteen-month-old daughter, named for Caroline Shaw, from the Sackville Street Mission.

Rosalie stayed near her children during the first weeks of that summer, pitching her tent just across the trail. She would lie in the grass outside the fence, listening to them in their play, distressed whenever the baby happened to cry. Then, soon after Elizabeth's return to the Mission, the tent disappeared, and Rosalie was gone for days.

Her absence was only another indication that the Indians from many Reserves were meeting at Deer Creek, about forty miles away, for the ceremony they called the Thirst Dance but that was more often named the Sun Dance. It was forbidden by law, ostensibly because of the mutilation sometimes practised; but there was deep religious significance in the Dance, and the Indians continued to gather secretly for it. If the Police did come to investigate, scouts warned the dancers, and they melted away, leaving no evidence save the lodge of poplar poles and saplings, and the circle marked by shuffling feet in the three days and two nights of the dance.

Men and women came to fulfill vows or to offer petitions; and Rosalie was there, in a last despairing effort, to pray for her own health. Rain for the summer's growth was the general petition, and rain fell every day of that ceremony. Rosalie danced until she was exhausted, or sat swaying to the beat of the drums and the chanting, while her clothes dried on her body. Then the Dance ended, and the Indians wandered back to their Reserves.

John Grace had looked out in the early morning, and had seen Rosalie's tent sagging against the pasture fence. He walked down to see how she was, and found her too weak to stand. He strengthened the tent, sent her dry blankets, as well as food each day from the Mission—but Rosalie died within a week.

The short summer went swiftly for Elizabeth, the weeks more restful than she had found in other years. Caroline Shaw was happy in the full-time occupation that the Mission offered, and was able to take charge of all the school sewing. The work was well advanced, and the number of children increased steadily.

When the holidays ended, Elizabeth could return to her studies with her mind at ease for the first time. The three little girls were to remain with their father, in the care of two competent women. They were happy children, united in a lively kinship that included the other children too, who in turn responded with spirit to the vibrant activity of a large family that they accepted as their own.

In that assurance, Elizabeth found herself ready for the challenge of her final year in Medicine.

Fifteen

Toronto was no longer a strange city to Elizabeth. She had friends among her classmates, and in the Deaconess Training House where she spent her Christmas holidays. Her work was going well. Then early in January 1898, she developed severe tonsilitis. Dr. Wishart at first suspected diphtheria and forbade her to study for five weeks. When her classmates visited her and found her disconsolate, they insisted that any one of them would feel certain of passing her examinations if Dr. Wishart forbade study; but it seemed to Elizabeth that she would lose her year, and her discouragement only increased.

The Head Deaconess persuaded some friends to take Elizabeth into their own comfortable and quiet home, that she might regain her strength and then concentrate on her work. The weeks proved well spent, and she returned with fresh vigour to her classes and to her practical work.

She was required to be student-in-charge at twelve maternity cases, and in two it was her good fortune to deliver twins. Since nursing was part of the training of the young deaconesses, she called upon them to assist her when she attended these maternity cases in the poorer sections of Toronto. Her patients appreciated the fact that she too had had experience in child-birth, and responded gratefully to her understanding, her skill and quickness.

In April 1898, she wrote and passed her examinations, receiving her degree as Doctor of Medicine from the University of Trinity College. When she left Toronto, she was accompanied by another volunteer for the Mission. Helen Marsh's gentle, sheltered life had scarcely prepared her for work in the North-West, yet she was to endear herself to Elizabeth as their difficult journey progressed.

They travelled as far west as Edmonton to meet John Grace, and arrived just at break-up, the river jammed with ice. Matheson had sent word to Donald Ross, and they were to stay at his house; but bad weather had delayed John Grace's wagons on their long cold trip from Onion Lake. Elizabeth and Helen Marsh had to wait in Strathcona, on the south bank, for two days. Then Ross came for them in a rowboat, and they crossed the surging muddy water through floating ice.

The wagons brought bales of good furs, and John Grace gave hours of each day to shrewd bargaining at the warehouses and mills. It had been Elizabeth's expectation that he would take the two women down the river on one of the scows, but he refused to consider it, for the spring of 1898 was most unpromising. They would have to drive to Onion Lake with Joe Quinney, taking the horses and wagon back to the Mission.

Winter clung obstinately to the river, and snow lay in discoloured drifts in every poplar bluff. The trail was rough, glazed with ice each morning; and twenty to thirty miles made a long day's trip for the horses and for the chilled travellers. They would camp for lunch, stop sometimes in mid-morning and afternoon "to boil tea", and at night stay at whatever shelter a stopping-place or shack might offer.

Helen Marsh accepted the rough hospitality with gentle graciousness; but at night, when they lay on the floor or on straw mattresses over the poles of a make-shift bed, Elizabeth would hear her sigh, or shiver involuntarily, and would think, "She must know there are bugs." In the morning, she would help to shake their blankets vigorously before they put the bedrolls into the wagon, without comment; but as the cheerless days passed, the gentle conversation that had been framed for drawing-rooms fell more and more into uncomplaining silence.

At Paradis Crossing, the ice had piled up on the banks, and Joe had to cut footholds in it for the horses to climb, and then whip them forward, stumbling as they jerked the lurching wagon to the top.

From the telegraph station at Moose Creek, Elizabeth sent word to the Mission, and home seemed near at last. Then heavy snow began to fall about them, obscuring everything, and Joe had to walk at the horses' heads, feeling out the trail while Elizabeth drove.

At the vague outline of tents, he gave a shout of relief. It was an encampment of Indians, muskrat trappers; and the travellers were cheerfully welcomed into the first tent, the inmates crowding over to give them room, pressing hot mugs of tea upon them.

Elizabeth watched how Miss Marsh cupped her hands gratefully about the warmth, but hesitated to drink; and then, with sudden resolution lifted the chipped enamel rim to her lips and sipped the scalding bitter brew with gentle composure. With rueful understanding, Elizabeth thought—Toronto, tea with her friends, beautiful china, soft voices, gracious manners?—and felt her own disappointment throb again, for this was not the home-coming to which she had looked forward either.

But the storm was clearing, and Joe was ready to go on. The horses plodded forward, pulling heavy wheels clogged with wet snow; then suddenly they were out of the snow, into the unexpected warmth of the sun, to find that winter's last attack had stopped short of the Mission.

At a turn in the trail, they saw the children, all of them, running to meet the wagon, shouting with laughter as Joe pulled the horses to a stop, then lifting up over the wheels five small excited girls—Elizabeth's and Rosalie's. In their hands, they clutched their gift for her, the first flowers of spring, the prairie crocuses.

Sixteen

It was late in May before John Grace could run his scows down the river to Mellon's landing; and as soon as the Mission had resumed its normal routine, he had to leave again to attend Synod in Prince Albert.

He was away most of June. These long trips were made usually only once a year, but he travelled regularly to the other Reserves in his charge, and he and his brother exchanged visits at the Battleford Industrial School or at the Mission every few months.

For Edward Matheson, the one-way trip of a hundred miles meant always three days of travelling; for John Grace, seldom more than two, now that he had good horses again. It was a difference that was reflected in all the coordination of their work and in their lives—the younger brother methodical and slow-moving, the elder impetuous, satisfied only with activity that demanded his full exertion; the one unhurried, giving meticulous attention to each small detail, the other driving himself, looking always for immediate results.

Within six years at the Mission the results of John Grace's energy and initiative were clear. The horses were only one indication, and, if part of his pleasure in them was that of a shrewd horse-trader, Elizabeth's delight was in driving and riding again as she had not done for years. His eyes would light with pride in both horse and driver. "You'll have the finest in the country, Bess, if I have my way."

Their cattle too had become a small herd, supplying the needs of the

Mission with dairy products and beef. He had had to secure permission to keep any, for the land was part of the Reserve; and all the hay had to be cut by government permit on lands outside.

Surveys in the area north of the Saskatchewan River would not be completed for some years, but Matheson had begun to plan a ranch on land a few miles down river from the site of Fort Pitt, near Frenchman's Butte, where he could prove his claim later to a quarter-section and lease three adjacent quarters from the government. It was good ranching country, and he was eager to make the venture, quite certain that with a capable foreman there would be profit in the cattle trade as settlement developed.

It seemed to Elizabeth, when she returned each summer, that however rapidly his plans took shape, the Mission grew even faster. There were forty children in 1898, and only ten of these were Treaty Indians who received grants once they reached school-age. But it was not only Rosalie's two sons and two daughters who were under age when John Grace accepted them. Sāna (Sarah) Chevasse was still a baby when she came. She remained until she was eighteen. Her mother was an Indian woman, blind and abandoned by her Metis husband. The Department finally agreed to allow rations for Sāna and then a grant before she had reached the required age.

The children, and not the government policy, were of greater concern to John Matheson as he enlarged the Mission House room by room to accommodate increasing numbers, while extending his trade to finance the work.

After Edward Matheson assumed the principalship of the Battleford Industrial School, some of its more capable senior pupils came to work at the Mission for a few months, some for even years at a time. Matilda Black had been the first, and she stayed for more than three years before she married Charles Trottier and went to his farm in a Metis settlement in the area. In 1898, James Brown came from the School. His training had made him a skilled carpenter, and he was able to help in the building, as well as in the outside work of the Mission.

When Elizabeth returned from Toronto with Helen Marsh, the work of the school-room and household could be shared by four women. The situation was not easy however. For three years, Annie Phillips had been in charge. There was no doubt about her competence and her dedication to the work, but the authority that she exercised produced an often heady mixture, since all her previous training had been in respectful obedience to orders.

Elizabeth had been making her own decisions from the time she was fourteen and had left her parents' home. She was a few years older than Miss Phillips, much more experienced, and better educated. More than that, she acted within her rights, both as John Matheson's wife and as an equal partner with him in this venture which they had initiated together. Nothing could take that from her. Even her absence of three years for further training had been part of their joint undertaking.

When she had left the Mission in 1895, it had been with deep reluctance, feeling the pain of separation from all that was most dear to her. Each summer she had been aware of change; yet she had convinced herself that when she completed her course and returned to stay, life would be as it had been before, with the same sense of shared achievement that had sustained her even in the lonely separation of her studies.

That could not be. There was change not only in the increased demands of the work, in the often presumptuous intrusion of Annie Phillips, but also within herself, the result of her stimulating association with other women, and her intensive medical training. During the first months neither seemed to have immediate relevance to life at the Mission, nor any validity.

She set up her dispensary and ordered the essential drugs to prepare her own medicines; but recognition as a doctor would come to her only gradually, and for the first year and more would be limited to the school. The Indians still preferred their own ways, and were fearful of any others; the Mounted Police, the Government and Hudson's Bay Company employees were strong young men usually, and if an emergency arose, they would telegraph for the doctor at Battleford. After all the new doctor was a woman.

Elizabeth was lost between two worlds, her medical training seldom required, her former position in the work of the Mission too often usurped by Miss Phillips. When Elizabeth objected she found herself invariably placed in the wrong. Miss Phillips was a dedicated worker; she had gained general respect. ("One fit to be the wife of a Bishop," Archdeacon J. A. Mackay declared.) The incidents that too often roused Elizabeth's quick impatience were small presumptions, and when her anger flared, it would be met with meekness and surprised denial. Elizabeth was made to feel a disturber of the peace, aware that John Grace was ashamed of her angry impatience and that he regarded it as quite unreasonable.

She had changed, he declared. Where was the eager response to every challenge, the ready wit and laughter, the former happiness of their work together? And Elizabeth could only ask herself the same questions. Had those attributes too been taken from her, assumed by another, so that her role could be only a secondary one? Or had she really changed? Was it the company of young students, interested in their work but sharing the normal interests and dreams of youth, that had wakened this yearning in her for a life of her own, not this negation, this constant, demanding absorption in the lives of others?

For the first time, she considered her husband from that aspect, and realized that for him youth was past and that he had lived it as completely as he now gave himself in these later years to the work of the Mission. The plume of white hair against the fading auburn of his head lent distinction to his handsome person, but for all his virile strength, John Grace was fifty.

She was thirty-two. In the seven years of their marriage, she had given herself without reservation to their work, had borne three children, had successfully completed as many years of difficult study—and in the end was isolated, unable to understand herself or be understood, ashamed of her jealousy, yet torturing herself with it.

Out of their friendship for Elizabeth, both Caroline Shaw and Helen Marsh tried to help her; but Caroline was not always discreet in what she revealed or advised, for she was young and in love herself, looking forward to the time when Donald Campbell would have completed his term of service with the North-West Mounted Police, and they could marry. Miss Marsh, who was past her youth, was too gentle and yielding to understand Elizabeth's strong-willed nature and her torment; and to her, the only answer lay in prayer and in Christian forbearance.

For Elizabeth, there would always have to be a physical outlet, and the more unhappy she felt, the harder she worked, driving herself until she was alarmingly thin and tired, quite unable to cope patiently with any problem.

If the situation was an unhappy one for Annie Phillips, she gave no indication, for she remained at the Mission for another six years, her evangelical zeal unabated, and her dedication to Indian work constant. In 1904, when James Brown returned to the Mission from his studies in theology at St. John's College in Winnipeg, they were married, and began their long journey by trail and river to his charge at Grand Rapids.

As their wagon moved away, wedding guests, members of staff, and children thronged forward to wave good-bye; but Elizabeth stepped back into the shadow of the hallway where John Grace stood quietly watching. He put his arms tightly around her. "Thank God," he said, with surprising intensity, "thank God, that woman's gone."

Seventeen

In 1898, when winter closed in around the Mission, Elizabeth's depression increased as she entered her fourth pregnancy. It was to be one of almost constant ill-health, with none of the joyous well-being that she had experienced before, only the blackness of despondency. They were months that became ever more difficult to endure, as she moved deeper into a darkness of spirit; for, to her mental torment was added increasing physical distress as pressure upon the sciatic nerve filled her days and nights with pain.

One Sunday morning, after a sleepless night, she found that she could scarcely move; but she had made her resolve, and waited until everyone had gone to the Cree service at the church and the house was deserted. In a locked cupboard in her dispensary, she had the means to end the torment finally, with her life. She found the key and crawled painfully to the dispensary. She unlocked the cupboard, and then, lying before it, fought again her battle with the powers of darkness, and knew at last that she could not bring herself to this final admission of defeat, this desperate act that would strike too against all those she loved.

In the empty stillness of the house, she dragged herself back to her room and to her bed. She heard the congregation returning from the service and the quick rush of her children's feet running to find her, to tell her eagerly all the excitement of that hour—how poor crazed Oo-ni-ka-moos (the Singer) had smoked her pipe in church, and how when Papa went down to where she sat on the floor at the back and told her that she must not smoke her pipe in church, she had laid it down and pounded it to pieces with her hatchet; but they had all sung as loudly as they could to cover the noise, and had kept their places. Then Oo-ni-ka-moos had left the church, muttering angry words, and frightening the other women. No one, not even one of the men, would have dared stop her. And she had laid the old blackened tea-pail that she always carried, on a stone just outside the door, and had smashed it flat. Now she was trying to push it back into shape; but Papa was looking for a new pail for her, and another pipe, and some tobacco. And how did Mamma feel? And Mamma, a little breathless too, her forehead still damp from her own ordeal, said that she felt better, that soon she would be well again.

For spring had come at last, and release from the long winter. The pain subsided, and she could move more readily, spending hours in the sunshine of her garden, directing the work she was not able to do herself.

She had planned that garden from her first year at the Mission, choosing a plot near the house, beside the trail along which they had come originally, that she might capture there again some of the loveliness of that first golden evening. It was light sandy soil that required stable manure and loam from the bush to enrich it, brought sometimes by the labour of man and horse, more often by wheelbarrows propelled by laughing boys.

George Mann had sent Elizabeth seedlings of Manitoba maple from the Agency, and tiny spruce trees had come from the ravines in the hills. Mrs. P. G. Laurie sent her a lilac all the way from the garden of *The Saskatchewan Herald* in Battleford. And Elizabeth had ordered shrubs from the government nurseries at Indian Head, artemesia for a hedge, and some caragana that she left untrimmed, to grow into trees that were thick with yellow bloom each spring. There were red, black and white currant bushes, and a wild honeysuckle that she had staked when it was in bloom, and then transplanted at the proper season. Sometimes the garden knew the flash of a humming-bird, and all summer long the drone of bumble-bees. There were common-place beds of rhubarb and onions for the kitchen; but there were flowers too, mignonette, and candy-tuft, and sweet william. And the fence about it all was no longer of poplar rails, but of neat pickets that recalled the gardens of her childhood in Ontario. In the place where she had planted beauty, she found healing too.

When summer holidays came, there was other occupation that also gave her release. Many of the children had joined their parents in summer camps, leaving only those who had no other home than the Mission, and a few older boys and girls who remained to help with the work.

In the children's dining-room, the floor was scrubbed bone-white, the tables pushed back to the windows, and Elizabeth had space for the work that she had planned for months, the making of two fur robes. For one of them John Grace had given her twenty-eight prime badger-skins, evenly marked, tipped with clear black. The other one was to be made of "cats' paws"—an unusual robe even then, perhaps one of the last ever made.

When a trapper skinned a lynx, he sometimes cut off the paws first, which made a quicker job of skinning as long as the buyer paid no attention, although the Hudson's Bay Company was refusing to take such skins.

The women would skin these paws and save the soft pieces of fur, which measured seldom more than four by six inches, depending on the size of the paw and how high up the leg the trapper had cut. It was slow work to save enough to make a robe, but small collections came in trade to John Grace, and he gave these to Elizabeth, as a curiosity. She might never have had the three hundred that she needed for a large robe if a woman in the Edmonton district had not learned of her interest, and sent her about one hundred and fifty, sewn together. There were pieces to spare then, and the poorer ones could be discarded.

Elizabeth sent for Isabel, who had clear vision in only one eye, but was still the finest needlewoman on the Reserve; and Isabel came, her moccasins beautifully beaded, her black skirts trimmed with row upon row of bright ribbons and dome fasteners that sparkled like sequins in the sunlight where she sat on the floor, hour after hour, stitching the pieces of fur together with fine sinew and waxed linen thread.

Elizabeth sat at a table, trimming the pieces exactly, cutting the scalloped flannel edging for both robes, making the linings of red blanket cloth that the Hudson's Bay Company sold by the yard for capotes and leggings.

The two women worked together, talking in Cree—Elizabeth pleased to find how easily the words came to her; and she worked even longer hours than Isabel, refusing to admit weariness, always unsatisfied until a job was finished. When the linings and edgings were ready, the badger pelts trimmed, she sat watching Isabel stitch together the last of the cats' paws.

John Grace had come into the room, and stood looking at the work. "Bits and pieces. Now these badger skins are good whole skins. You'll have something to show for your work there."

And Elizabeth, seeing the reverse side only of the skins, spread like a drab patchwork across the floor, repeated the words. Bits and pieces. That's what it did seem in fact, despite all Isabel's fine work. Like her own life so far. A piece of this, a piece of that, teacher, missionary, wife, mother, and now doctor. Even if she had the skill to put it all together, would it be much more than patchwork in the end?

But Isabel stood up, lifting a corner of the robe in her dark-skinned hand. "Lift it with me," she said to John Grace, "and you will see the robe we've made for Mu-skē-kē-s-quāu."

Elizabeth heard her new name, Medicine-woman, spoken as naturally and simply as that. She watched them lift the patchwork of skins, reversing it on the table. She caught her breath. Sunlight, streaming through the window, glinted across the silvery hairs, and the patchwork was lost in one shimmering robe, whole and perfect.

Eighteen

When the Mathesons came to the Mission in 1892, there was no well. In summertime, the Taylors had used water from a slough outside the grounds, and carried drinking water from one of the Agency wells. Within the first weeks, John Grace had dug a well just beyond the house, striking good water at thirty-five feet; and when the house was extended, he built a room around the well, with a short passage to connect it to the kitchen. It was safely cribbed, with a box-like structure over the mouth of the well, and a pulley for the bucket.

Each summer, when holidays had emptied the school, and the water in the well was low, it was thoroughly cleaned and then limed. James Brown and Fred Ballendine were assigned the work that summer. They had removed the upper structure and drawn all the remaining water; then from a ladder against the lower casing, had begun scraping the cribbing in preparation for liming.

When the noon hour came and they were called to dinner, they left the well as it was. It seemed quite safe. Everyone else was supposedly at dinner, except Bella Okanese, and she had come from the hot kitchen to sit in a corner of the cool room, with some chickens she was plucking. She would be on guard until the men returned.

They were gone only a few minutes when Riema came running past the door of the well-room, with all the single-minded purpose of a five-year-old with great news to tell. She saw Bella, and turned at once through the doorway, obeying the quick warning and stepping cautiously away from the open well, but with no clear awareness, intent only upon her news. She had found the turkey-hen's nest, far in a corner of the pasture, hidden by the fence. "It's big," she cried. "A big, big nest. This big." She swept her arms in a circle, and stepped back, back into the mouth of the well, plunging down into darkness.

Bella's scream brought the men racing from the table. All she could say was "Riema!" and point to the well. There was no other sound. Brown was the smallest of the three men. "I'll lower you," Matheson said, indicating the rope and pulley . He noticed the young man's agitation, and in the same dull level voice added, "I'll put you down slowly. There's no need to hurry." The child's quavering voice called then, "Oh, do hurry, Papa. It's cold down here."

As Brown made his quick descent, the lantern above threw his shadow against the walls. His eyes searched the bottom of the well. "There's nothing here, Mr. Matheson," he called, and then heard beside him the puzzled voice of the child. "Here I am."

She had climbed part way up the ladder set against the lower casing, and clung there by one hand. Her other arm was broken, her head was cut, and blood streamed from a gash in her thigh. Brown held her to him, and they were pulled to the surface. John Grace took her into his arms and carried her from the room. Elizabeth had been resting, and had not heard the commotion. "Get her mother," he said; but Annie Phillips was there first, and when Elizabeth came, she was holding the little girl, crying over her, uttering tearful sympathy.

It was a touching scene of tender mother love, and the true mother had to say coldly, "Lay her down. Leave her alone while I examine her." Calmly she set the broken arm in splints, bandaged the gashed thigh and cut head. "You'll be all right now, N'tanis," she whispered, and stroked the small white face. The child opened her eyes, blue as her father's. "Oh, Mamma, I found the turkey's nest."

That was on July 3rd. On July 17th Elizabeth gave birth to her fourth daughter. Two Indian women attended her. She had expected only one, a woman whose husband, John Bangs, was interpreter and labourer at the Agency; but Mrs. Bangs was shy, and asked if she might bring her husband's mother too, the widow of a noted Cree warrior, The Hawk.

The birth was normal; the child dark-eyed, dark-haired, in contrast to the fairness of her sisters. They named her Helen Grace, for her Godmother Helen Marsh, and for her father. Her mother would remember always her own tormented unsettling pregnancy, and would relate it to the variable temperament of the child.

Officials of the Department of Indian Affairs were at the Agency that day to make payments, according to the Treaty of 1876: "to each Indian person the sum of Five Dollars per head yearly . . . each Chief, duly recognized as such . . . an annual salary of twenty-five dollars per annum; and each subordinate officer, not exceeding four each Band . . . fifteen dollars per annum."

Indians from the Reserves in the Agency had assembled to present themselves by families for the Treaty payments, registering any children born since the payments of the previous year. Encampments had sprung up in every clearing about the Agency and the Missions, and traders too had appeared.

The weather had been hot, and in the morning a storm broke, with violent winds and a cloudburst of rain that tore the tents down, destroying new as well as old, and flooding the Mission yard. From everywhere the people ran for shelter, crowding into the Mission buildings, to stay all day while their women mended the torn canvas or made new tents.

When a group of families moved on to the Agency for their payments, John Grace joined them, presenting himself at the Agent's table as the line moved forward. "Come to register a child," he said. "Born on this Reserve, and can't speak a word of English." "Name!" George Mann snapped. "Why Matheson, of course. A daughter. Born this morning." It was a story that would be repeated all through the encampments, with mirth that lightened the morning's disaster.

Elizabeth's strength returned only slowly this time, but before the summer had passed, she welcomed the opportunity to drive to Battleford.

Two new members had been recruited on staff at the Industrial School, both on her recommendation. The first was her own brother, Jim Scott, who had come from New Westminster in February, to be the farming instructor. Elizabeth had not seen him since the time when he had reluctantly accepted her marriage to John Matheson.

In the years since then, her only contact with her family had been through letters. Her father had died; and it was Tom who seemed closest to her. He had completed his course in Medicine, had married Mary MacCallum, and with her was establishing the hospital at Manepay in Ceylon. The letters between him and his sister were more than mere communications. They could write of their work and of their lives in terms that both understood, sustaining their affection and interest in each other.

Apart from Tom, Elizabeth had identified herself wholly with the Mathesons, drawn into the closely knit relationship of John Grace's people. It was out of concern for Edward Matheson that her second recommendation had been given, resulting in Eleanor Shepphird's arrival in June at Battleford as a member of staff from the Deaconess Training House in Toronto. The work of the House had appealed to Elizabeth, and she had urged Edward Matheson to request a trained deaconess for the Battleford School. Their training was intensive, modelled upon Mildmay House in England, and Kaiserwert in Germany, where Florence Nightingale had trained.

The first Toronto graduates had entered into parish work in that city, or had gone to foreign missions, particularly to China, where Bishop White of the Diocese of Honan had lamented: "How can they speak out against the bound feet of Chinese women and wear tight lacings themselves that bind their own waists and bodies?"

Eleanor Shepphird's waist measured only eighteen inches, her shoes were size three-and-a-half, and she was scarcely five feet in height. But in their friendship at the Deaconess House Elizabeth had called her "Miss Indepen-

Eleanor Shepphird (*c.* 1885).

dence''. It was that quality that was unexpected in one so small and gentle: evidence of great spiritual strength, of quiet maturity and purpose.

She had been a little older than the others in training. And Elizabeth had seen how the younger girls turned to Eleanor Shepphird with their problems, and how even the Head Deaconess had depended upon her. The practice work she undertook was amongst the poor of Toronto, who received her with affection. It was healing and peace that she brought with her, understanding, and the warmth of wit and laughter.

The situation in the Battleford School was an unhappy one at the time, for Ray Matheson's third child had died in infancy, and it was evident that her own health was failing. She was scarcely able to make even the contribution in music that had endeared her to the pupils of the school, and Edward Matheson carried the heavy responsibility almost single-handed.

At St. Barnabas Mission, the boarding-school was simply an extension of the principal's home; and Edward would have developed the same sense of family in the larger institution. It had seemed to Elizabeth that one of the young deaconesses might give the warmth and feeling of a home to the life of the school, but she had not dared hope that the response to Edward's appeal would be the loving bright spirit of Eleanor Shepphird.

When they met at Battleford, she realized that she had almost forgotten how small Eleanor was, how trim and dainty. On sudden impulse, and without regard for the usual formality in names, Elizabeth put her arms around her. "You are Eleanor to me," she said. "Everyone else may call you Miss Shepphird, but that's not for us anymore. You need me, but how much more do I need you."

They walked together through the sparsely furnished rooms, the bare halls, to the room assigned this newest member of staff; and at her first glimpse as the door was opened, Elizabeth gave way to laughter. There it was—not the bleakness for which she was prepared, but the serene aspect of a remembered world—crisp curtains at the window, monogrammed linen towels, embroidered pillow-shams and table runners, a bowl of fresh flowers. "O Toronto! O Eleanor! I might have known it. You'll stay amongst us, but on your own terms. Dear Miss Independence, you'll make your corner Toronto for as long as you live with us."

They laughed together, and Elizabeth found that to be able to laugh at themselves and the foolishness of others, to have Eleanor Shepphird's understanding friendship, to be even this near to her gave her strength. She returned to the Mission refreshed.

Nineteen

John Bangs was Elizabeth's first patient from outside the school, and he came to her dispensary simply to have a tooth pulled. He had been having trouble with it, he told her, and he wanted it out. Soon he and James Slater, the farm instructor, would be taking the Agency cattle up into the northern bush, where abundant hay was ready and there was good shelter. The wintering camp where Bangs would be stationed was seventy-five miles to the north-west, and tooth-ache under those conditions could be a calamity.

The tooth that was troubling him was a molar, apparently sound and well-rooted; and he was a giant of a man. Elizabeth agreed to try to pull it if he, on his part, would promise not to grab at the forceps.

He sat on a straight-backed chair, and gripped the seat in his powerful hands. Elizabeth found the proper forceps and clamped them about the tooth, trying first to loosen it with her right hand. Bangs did not move, but neither did the tooth. She put both hands to the forceps, twisting the tooth, tugging hard. He grunted encouragingly. She stopped for a moment to catch her breath, then took a fresh grip on the forceps, braced her knee against the chair, and gave a sharp twist and a quick strong pull on the forceps. The molar tore loose with a sudden wrench that flung her quite off balance to the floor. When she scrambled to her feet, flushed and triumphant, the tooth held high in her forceps, Bangs responded with a wide and bloody grin—no more tooth, no more trouble.

Late in October there was trouble at the wintering camp on Long Lake Creek, when young Philip Bangs slipped as he was climbing the log fence of the corral, and broke his leg.

His father rode out to the station at Moose Creek to telegraph for the doctor, and the operator at Onion Lake sent the telegram down to the Mission in the early afternoon.

Elizabeth read it and made no comment when she passed it to John Grace. That trail to the camp on Long Lake Creek was cut through bush and across muskeg where logs were laid to make a "corduroy" road, rough and difficult at any season, but frozen hard now, for the weather had turned bitterly cold, and no snow had yet fallen.

John Grace said slowly, "It could be a hard trip at this time of the year, and you'd have the baby with you." She hesitated only a moment. "Impossible for the boy. I'll make a try." "That's my Bess." His voice was relieved.

It would have to be the heavy lumber wagon for that trail; it had a new spring seat and there would be a strong fresh team, as well as Albert Fraser to drive her.

Fraser had come to the Mission only that summer, but he was not new to the West, for he was a grandson of Colin Fraser, piper to Sir George Simpson on his famous journeys. John Grace had known the family for years, and when the young man had come from Athabasca Landing to Edmonton, he had brought him down the river on one of the scows, enlisting him for work at the Mission. It was a turning point in Fraser's life, and the inspiration of John Matheson's example was to strengthen his own work as a missionary in later years in other areas of the Diocese.

100

Elizabeth knew that except for John Grace himself she could have no better driver than young Albert Fraser, and his company would relieve the monotony of the long drive.

They would take her new robes with them—"a chance to handsel the cat's paw and the badger." John Grace looked at that grey sky, sensed the chill wind. They'd have to be on the trail as soon as possible if they were to reach Frog Lake before night. He urged them not to go any farther than Slater's camp the next day. They could make the camp with an early start in the morning from Frog Lake. The last fifteen miles of the trip would be the hardest, and they'd need rested horses and daylight to make Bangs's camp.

Elizabeth was ready when they drove the horses to the door, and she took her place on the spring-seat, fur-robes under and about her, the infant in its snug moss-bag, secure in her arms. She wore her new jacket of Persian lamb, fashionably close-fitting, with its high storm collar protecting her face, and the matching cap pulled down about her ears and forehead. Her long skirts of wool serge and her trim moccasins were warm and comfortable.

The rush of preparation, the excitement of her first medical case outside the school had restored lively spirit to the remarkable eyes that lit her whole face with beauty. "You'll make it, Bessie," her husband said with pride.

The horses went at a strong and steady pace, the seat springing only lightly as the wagon moved along the Frog Lake trail; when darkness fell they camped in an Indian's house. At day-break they were on their way again, and the trail grew steadily worse as it led through bush, skirting muskeg and the thin ice of freezing lakes.

Elizabeth began to tire. Her slight body ached from the constant jolting along the frozen rutted trail, and her arms were tense about the child. There was little talk, only the sound of horses' feet striking the unyielding earth, the moaning of the wind in bare branches, and now and then the wakeful cry of the infant.

She found herself measuring the miles to the first wintering camp, to the cheerful welcome that hearty Mrs. Slater would extend. The grey day darkened into night, and she watched intently for the light from the shack. Then, even as it shone to greet them, a figure detached itself from the shadow of a dark spruce, a huge man on a shaggy horse, looming centaur-like in the dimness. John Bangs had ridden out from his camp to meet them.

The trail for the next fifteen miles was bad, he explained in his deep-throated Cree, and he had come to guide them; but Elizabeth, seeing that beckoning light, feeling her own weariness, knew what had prompted him to waylay them. She nodded to Fraser. They went on without turning, and the light from Slater's camp lost itself again in the darkening bush that closed in about them.

They followed Bangs mile after mile over the frozen corduroy road. The tired horses picked their stumbling way; the wagon jolted and lurched over logs; and high above their heads the northern lights flashed ice-cold.

Elizabeth thought of the Indian belief that these were the undaunted spirits of warriors who had died in battle. Sometimes, with vivid colours, they would foretell disaster and terror on earth. More often, as that night, they leaped in icy green to blue, remote in triumph, far above the earth's pain, the happy brave, moving in graceful dance that mocked all stumbling endurance of the earth-bound.

The cold crept in about the wagon. Fraser, young and tired, dozed fitfully. Elizabeth's own eyes were heavy, but she dared not close them, guarding her child. The same uneasiness troubled Bangs. Whenever he could, he rode beside her, a great bulk, silent except when his deep rumbling voice warned, "There's a low branch," and again, "The trail's high just ahead. Keep the horses to the middle."

To Elizabeth, in a tired half-stupor, it seemed to be all without end, the weariness and the darkness of the night merging into the conflict in which she had wandered for months, as though in overcoming one that night, she could win a double victory.

It was late when they reached the shack, and the cold was numbing. They were grateful for the supper that Mrs. Bangs had kept hot; but, as soon as she could, Elizabeth turned her attention to the patient, and directed the father to make the proper splints. Philip was laid on the table, a coal-oil lantern hanging above to throw some light on his leg; and Fraser was shown how to administer chloroform.

The fracture proved to be a simple one of the left femur, but the leg was badly swollen. The doctor had just begun her careful manipulation when Fraser staggered away from the table, out into the cold of the night, sick with the smell of chloroform. Nervously, Mrs. Bangs came to take his place, only to scream at the first sight of her boy's still face—"He's dead. My son's dead"—and to stumble to the door, half-fainting. She crouched there upon the step, her lips quivering into the keening wail of her people, old as human grief, the voice of Rachel mourning.

Elizabeth shut the door firmly. The splints were ready. Bangs would have to give the chloroform, drop by careful drop. He took his place at the boy's head, and then suddenly stammered that he would have to stop. Elizabeth's eyes flashed green fire. All she said was, "Do as I've told you!" and he bent his great bulk sharply to the job, his face darkly flushed by the whip-lash of her voice. But when they had finished, and the last splint was secure, she smiled at him, "We've done a good job, you and I," and met his grateful eyes.

She laid herself then beside her baby in the fur-robes, to be lost in the same sound sleep until dawn came and the return trip could begin. Fraser had decided to make Middle Creek their objective that day, where Louis Patenaude and his sons were trapping muskrat. Their shack would offer shelter for the night.

It was quite dark when they arrived, but at the sound of wheels and the thud of horses' hooves on the frozen earth, Louis flung open the door. At once he recognized the travellers, and welcomed them with all the excited cheerfulness of Gallic unrestraint, bringing his sons in a tumbling rush to the low door to take the baby, to help the doctor alight, to stable the horses.

In the chill of bleak surroundings, the kindness of these rough men shone with surprising gallantry. Anything, anything was hers, Louis insisted. Let her take the bed that night, the only bed. They would sleep on the floor. No, not that, she told him; her robes were soft and comfortable. Just give her a corner to spread them, and nothing would keep her from sleep that night.

Her sleep, however, was not quite undisturbed. Once she heard Louis's cheerful statement, "Just me and my sons and the doctor. Plenty of room," and in the dimness distinguished the black cassocks of two Roman Catholic priests entering the shack. And through the night, came other indistinct voices, Cree, English, French; drafts of cold air from the opening door; soft moccasined steps about the room. Only in the morning did she learn how many had found the same shelter that night, for there were eighteen of them in all, including the priests and three Indian families.

Before it was quite light, she and Fraser left. The road was just visible in a greyness of earth and sky before the coming storm. When they reached Clearwater Lake, still twenty miles from the Mission, snow was falling heavily. It cumbered the wheels of the wagon, slowing the straining horses to a walk. The dwelling of Ka-mis-tu-tim (The Horse) was not far from the trail, and he would have a sleigh to lend them. Before Fraser turned the horses from the trail, however, he found the shelter of a poplar bluff for Elizabeth, and lit a fire there with the tea-pail swinging from a tripod over it.

As she waited in the white stillness, and nursed her child, Elizabeth realized that the dark depression of months had lifted. She felt at peace, her discouragement and bitterness defeated, not only from without, from the evident respect of others for her work as a doctor, but from within, by the fulfillment of challenging duty, by restored life-preserving self-esteem.

Twenty

In 1899, Elizabeth Matheson was not registered to practise Medicine in the North-West Territories. But such lack of medical status was not unusual then, and when there was often no other practitioner within a hundred miles or more, it was generally condoned.

The College of Physicians and Surgeons of the North-West Territories had been created by ordinance in 1888. Its Council was to register any member of any incorporated College of Physicians and Surgeons or of any similarly organized body in the Dominion of Canada, or anyone with such qualifications as would entitle him to be registered by such a body—a clause intended to enable qualified men from Great Britain and Ireland to register without examination. Those presenting a diploma representing a four-year course in Medicine were also to be registered after an examination "if deemed necessary".

For Elizabeth, it was "deemed necessary", and she was informed that she would have to appear in Calgary for examination. Whether with justification or not, this seemed discriminatory to her, for she was convinced that two men, who had received their degrees from Trinity with her, had been registered without examination and were now practising in the Territories. Neither could she see why the work that she was doing at a Mission required registration under such conditions.

Nor, it would appear, did Dr. Seymour, Commissioner of Health for the Territories, when Elizabeth telegraphed Regina in February 1901, informing him of an outbreak of smallpox, and requesting authority to act. It came swiftly. She was appointed "Sanitary Inspector", and the Police were to assist her.

The first case to which she was called occurred in a Metis settlement just off the Reserve. Charlie Parenteau had a slight eruption on his face, enough to alarm those to whom smallpox was familiar, and who could remember fearful epidemics of earlier years.

Elizabeth had never seen smallpox during her student days; and Charlie had no fever or pain. She thought of varioloid, but diagnosed chicken-pox. Then a few days later, George Young developed a rash, with high fever and intense pain in his back; and she knew it was smallpox—and in their very midst, for Young was stableman at the Mission.

Caroline Shaw was next. Although every effort was made to quarantine, it was difficult under the circumstances, and forty cases developed in the school. Fortunately the disease lacked its former virulence, and there were no deaths; nor did it spread to the Reserves.

With the authority from Regina, Elizabeth visited every family, vaccinating anyone who could not show a satisfactory scar from previous vaccination. Sergeant Hall accompanied her, with William Sibbald, who was the new Indian Agent.

There were no more cases until the next spring, and these occurred off the Reserve again, at Baptiste Dumont's house on the river, ten miles away; at Red Deer, forty miles to the east; and at Island Lake, on Little Hunter's Reserve, away to the north. Each time, Sergeant Hall accompanied Elizabeth, and quarantine was enforced, the Agent supplying full rations to quarantined Indian families, the Mission helping to replace clothing and bedding that had to be burned before quarantine could be safely lifted.

In the late spring of 1901, when the epidemic at the Mission had subsided, a girl from the Reserve was brought to Elizabeth. Maria Cook had a heavy eruption on her face, and though the doctor was reasonably certain that it was not smallpox, she was taking no chances. A tent was pitched just across the trail from the Mission, and there Maria was installed, a solitary and reluctant captive.

Day after day, no other symptoms appearing, she sat disconsolate at the door of the tent; and day after day, as it happened, Johnny Heathen would ride by. He had been one of the boys in the school that first winter, and his liveliness always appealed to Elizabeth. The children would crowd to the fence whenever he appeared. His pony would cavort, slowing its canter as Johnny leaped off and on again. It was fascinating to watch his lithe grace and his tricks; and the entertainment brought some cheer to Maria's quarantine.

One morning, she did not appear at the door of her tent, nor did Johnny ride by. She had vanished in a night of moonlit wonder, had broken quarantine, had run away with Johnny up into the northern bush. There was nothing that Elizabeth could do.

Including Maria's dubious quarantine, the smallpox and its aftermath had lasted for almost five months. To Elizabeth, 1901 would always be "the year of the small-pox", and her own recollections would centre about that. And yet, in the midst of such concern, in May, she bore another child, Edith Eleanor.

Elizabeth was still a mother in every essential of love, but she had enlarged her scope as a woman, reaching out beyond her family and the Mission, accepting responsibility as a doctor in a wider area, and being accepted as such.

During these months of smallpox, the work of the school had been seriously hampered; and when John Matheson made his annual report to the Bishop, he acknowledged with gratitude gifts of clothing, bedding, and groceries sent from eastern branches of the Woman's Auxiliary to the Missionary Society, who were paying the salaries of Annie Phillips and Caroline Shaw as well.

He did not try to estimate the value of the goods that were sent, but in the receipts of the school he listed the money for those salaries and for his own, which had reached its maximum of $600. There was a new entry as well, of $100 "for medical services". That cheque had come from the Department of Indian Affairs, when Mr. Sibbald, the Agent, had drawn their attention to the presence of a qualified doctor at Onion Lake, and the extent of her unpaid work at a critical time. This official recognition was to continue in an annual salary of $300.

With these figures, John Matheson's financial statement included the total of the per capita grant from the Department for the seventeen children who were Treaty Indians; and the grant from the Territorial Government towards the salary of a teacher for the forty-two who were not. Then there were certain small donations to recognize, and these brought the total receipts to $2415.80—to finance the Mission for one year.

In order to meet such a small budget neither the principal nor the medical officer drew any salary for themselves. The other members of staff—and there were six that year—agreed to reductions in theirs, so that the payment for all six came to a total of $540. That, at least, was the sum which appeared in the statement; actually, John Matheson took the will for the deed more often, and made up in various ways for any sacrifice on the part of a staff member.

Before his yearly trip to Edmonton, he would learn the needs of each one, just as he received from his little girls their laboriously prepared list of purchases that they expected him to make for them. All these he tried to fill, whether it was a few yards or a bolt of certain material, a toy stove, tiny parasols, dolls' hats, or—the request of Annie Phillips—a fine English saddle. He paid the fees at Wycliffe College for Albert Fraser; he gave Miss Phillips her passage to England for a holiday.

These items, however, never appeared in any statement. John Matheson simply paid for them himself. He was quite sincere in his conviction that certain members of staff had made genuine sacrifice for the sake of the work; and he appreciated the faithfulness of that service.

Costs of equipment, building and repairs, fuel and light, provisions and clothing were listed; and they reflected the careful economy, the effort to make the Mission as self-sustaining as the family farms of the Red River Settlement had been in John Grace's boyhood. That policy, and the training it afforded in some degree to almost every child, in farm and household work, was common sense to him and Elizabeth. Only what could not be produced at the Mission was bought; and often through trade in kind when the Indians brought sleigh-loads of wood or frozen fish from northern lakes.

Only cash payments found their way into any statement to the Bishop, particularly for staples purchased in Edmonton, and without the estimated cost of bringing them down the river. Reduced in all these ways, the total expenditure still came to almost four thousand dollars in 1901, as against receipts of less than two thousand five hundred. Almost as a matter of course, John Matheson balanced the two with the item: "contributed from private sources . . . $1,453.05."

Even four thousand dollars came to less than $60 per pupil. At the Battleford Industrial School, Edward Matheson's equally careful management had reduced the cost from $186 to $160, which was lower than at Emmanuel College in Prince Albert, the third Indian boarding-school in the Diocese.

At Battleford and Prince Albert, the statements accounted for receipts large enough to meet careful expenditures in government-authorized schools. At Onion Lake, the Mission school was John Matheson's own venture; and his financial statement accounted for moneys that were only grants in aid. The actual cost per pupil, however, must have been approximately the same as in his brother's precise account. Which meant that it may have cost John Matheson himself one hundred dollars annually for every child that he accepted in the school.

The development of the Mission, and his methods of financing the project, had both progressed with such natural assurance that only strangers were puzzled, refusing often to believe that any man could give himself unselfishly to such work as a missionary without personal gain, and compete successfully with others as trader and builder and then as rancher too. Yet having undertaken the work of the Mission, he had really no choice but to continue; and Elizabeth knew the unceasing effort required to support what had become surely the largest family in all the North-West.

Twenty-One

The original log school-house had been long outgrown, and now served for other purposes. Classes were held on the lower floor of a two-storey building that John Grace had erected in 1898, of logs that had been brought down the river from Edmonton. Now he was planning a three-storey frame building, with a large class-room on the first floor, and staff rooms and boys' dormitories above; and he had brought an English carpenter on the scows from Edmonton to supervise the work. Every bit of lumber from the four scows that he ran down the river that summer, and every nail, would be used again at the Mission; and the scows had carried an extra load of lumber that would season over the winter.

When he went again to Edmonton, in the late summer, the scows that he built were to carry the usual supplies; but one was arranged for another purpose, to bring two passengers on as restful and pleasant a journey as possible. One was Miss Fanny Cross, who had had to retire from her position in Toronto as Head of the Deaconess House; and she was accompanied by her friend, Helen Marsh, who was returning as a voluntary worker to the Mission, and had persuaded Miss Cross to make this long journey in the hope that it might restore her health. Doctors in Toronto had agreed to this, though they knew that the gentle woman was dying of tuberculosis. No one in Toronto or at the Mission had thought of denying her the right to live freely amongst others, and to use her intellect and training as long as strength remained, in service to the young.

The Mission had interested Miss Cross since she had first met Elizabeth Matheson in Toronto. Had it been possible then, she might have volunteered as willingly as Helen Marsh. Instead it had been her cherished student, Eleanor Shepphird, who accepted the call to Battleford and that School's associated work.

When it was recognized that Miss Cross had not long to live, Eleanor made the hundred-mile drive in wintertime to nurse her loved friend. The gentle radiance of both patient and nurse had its effect throughout the Mission. Miss Cross instructed the older girls in Scripture as long as it was possible for her, while Eleanor appealed to the little ones in particular. Elizabeth's children called her "Aunt Eleanor", delighting in the foolish rhymes that she taught them, and in the quick turn of her Irish wit. And for Elizabeth too, there was refreshment in the company of her friends.

Another who came frequently to be with them was the Indian Agent's wife. William Sibbald was a gentleman, and his brother in Edinburgh was in fact titled. Mrs. Sibbald brought to the unaccustomed settlement all the gracious bearing of a Victorian lady—"the first lady of Onion Lake", she would calmly assert.

In that capacity, she made a call on Elizabeth one day. "I hear you're interesting again," she said, in the discreet euphemism of the day; and Elizabeth, well advanced into her sixth pregnancy, pretended ignorance of the term. "I flatter myself I always am."

Mrs. Sibbald was having no such evasion, and her tone changed. Bluntly she flashed, "By George, this has *got* to stop"; and Elizabeth retorted mildly, "But George had nothing to do with it, Mrs. Sibbald."

For her confinement, Elizabeth was assured the hands of a practised woman, the wife of James Slater, and the mother herself of five sons and three daughters. The Slaters had come originally from Red River, first to Prince Albert and Bresaylor and then to Onion Lake, where he was employed by the Agency. Their house overflowed with laughter and jig steps and tunes. All the children at the Mission delighted in Mrs. Slater. Whenever their play brought them to the hill at her door, they were eager to hear that warm "Red River bungay", and to receive thick slices of fresh home-made bread, rich with newly churned butter.

Her humour lightened even the hour of birth for Elizabeth in February, when their joint labour brought forth a son at last, named Selkirk Edward. Now Elizabeth was more than a step ahead of Sergeant Hall's wife.

That Irish gentleman—he became only more courteous with every drink, Elizabeth would recall—had married soon after the Mathesons came to Onion Lake; and had moved the Mounted Police barracks to larger quarters about three miles farther west along the Edmonton trail. His wife had produced four daughters, step by step with Elizabeth's second, third, fourth, and fifth. They compared their lot to that of the Czarina of all the Russias —one daughter after another—though all the world knew how vital it was that an heir should be born to that Imperial throne. But no one was particularly concerned about succession at the Police Barracks or the Anglican Mission.

At the Mission the joy of this birth was touched with sorrow as another life drew to its close in the sickroom where Fanny Cross lay. She died on Easter Saturday. Eleanor Shepphird was sadly released to return to Battleford, and there give her nursing skill to another sick woman. Edward Matheson's wife was dying of cancer.

The gentle deaconess had been distressed to see how much was required of Gladys in the work of the Mission, though she was only ten years old. Ever since the birth of her first sister, she had assumed responsibility in comforting and guiding each small child in turn. This was extended now in duties that she just as willingly assumed as her mother's assistant in the dispensary at the Mission.

Each morning, school children with sore eyes would lie in a row on the floor of that room, while the small nurse administered drops prescribed by the doctor; and then she gave cod-liver oil to the children as they advanced in a line to where she stood beside the bottle, spoon in hand. The boys, big and little alike, would move past her to the outer door, but not until each in turn had said, with slow formality, "T'ank you, G-nadys", so that she could be certain that each had swallowed the necessary but still repelling dose.

It seemed to Eleanor Shepphird that the child should have a holiday, and she suggested that Gladys be allowed to go to Battleford to stay at her uncle Jim Scott's home, and enjoy the company of his little girl of the same age. There was no hesitancy at the Mission. Gladys could have her holiday, the envy of every other child as she left on this rare adventure.

Charles Trottier would be their driver, and they would go by the winter trail on the north bank of the Saskatchewan River, the old Carlton trail, until they passed the confluence of the Saskatchewan and the Battle Rivers, crossing then to the School in the former government buildings, on the heights that overlooked both rivers and the town between them.

They left early one morning during Easter week, snow still lingering in patches, though the trail was bare and the grass dry enough to burn as the smoke of distant prairie fires indicated. On the second day of the trip, one of these fires swept towards them. Trottier turned his horses directly into it, and with wild shouts whipped them through the flames to the safety of burned-over ground. Smoke reddened the eyes of driver and passengers alike. Trottier wore a wide-brimmed Western hat; and Eleanor's hat had its brim too, above the thick-lensed glasses that her vision required. Gladys was wearing only a toque, but she made no particular complaint, either about the smoke or the glare of sun on white patches of snow, and it was not until the end of the day that either Trottier or the inexperienced young woman knew that she was suffering the acute distress of snow-blindness.

One mishap followed another. When they came to the river crossing, it was jammed with ice, and they had to lodge for a day and a night in a crowded house, where they slept on the floor. Bedbugs and fleas tormented the tired child, and she scratched her sensitive skin until it bled, her restlessness attributed to the misery of snow-blindness. All attention was given to the river and the crashing sound of ice as it gradually cleared.

A man had driven down from the school to meet them on the opposite bank, and waited there until they could be taken across in a rowboat through the last drifting ice. As they touched the muddy shore of the south bank, the man at the oars jumped out quickly, giving the boat a strong jerk that sent his unsuspecting passengers back into the shallow icy water. Immediate action brought them at a gallop to the warmth of the School.

During the weeks of that spring at Battleford, they were to witness a journey of such epic proportions that the trip from Onion Lake would seem only a small incident by comparison. The Barr Colonists were passing through Battleford on their way to homesteads and the town that they would establish and name Lloydminster. It was only thirty-five miles south of Onion Lake, and settlement would spread north of the river within a few years.

Some two thousand emigrants from the British Isles sailed from Liverpool on March 31, 1903, under the leadership of the Rev. Isaac Barr, who had secured an extensive land reservation for the Colony. He was capable enough in planning, but not in implementing the scheme; and when the colonists reached Battleford in May, there were angry demonstrations against him. The Rev. George Exton Lloyd was authorized to assume the leadership instead.

Independently of Barr's inept arrangements, the Canadian Government made plans to receive the colonists. When they arrived at Saskatoon, there was a temporary canvas city of about five hundred tents and marquees; and along the two hundred miles of trail to their settlement, some hills were graded and bridges built. But the journey still took weeks for many of the slow ox-drawn wagons, and was an ordeal that severely tested the endurance and resolution of the colonists.

Twenty-Two

With the establishment of the Barr Colony, other doctors came to the area. Elizabeth knew that she must secure registration, but the answer to her request was still the same. She would have to appear in Calgary for examination. She had been practising for five years, and any examination would require so thorough a review that she decided that she would be wiser to take her fourth year again in a Medical College. Manitoba was the logical choice.

Mabel Cassidy, a former classmate of hers at the Ontario Medical College for Women, was home on furlough from China, and readily agreed to serve as doctor at the Mission; and a deaconess, Ida Collins, joined the staff as well.

Elizabeth took her six-month-old son with her, and Gladys. It was time, her parents had decided, that the girl should have schooling beyond what was available at the Mission. In Winnipeg she would be free of all her other duties, even responsibility for her baby brother, who was placed in the care of a practical nurse at Baie St. Paul near Winnipeg.

Everyone was certain that Gladys would be happier in such circumstances—everyone but Gladys herself. Instead, she was utterly unhappy, lonely for her sisters, lonely for the thriving life of the Mission, lonely even for the duties that others had considered too much for a child.

Towards the end of September, her father had to come to Winnipeg on business; two young women were going back with him to Onion Lake, one to be the teacher. It was not difficult for Gladys to persuade him to take her home again. Everyone there had missed her, and he more than any other.

When he left Winnipeg on the return journey, John Matheson had a cold; at Saskatoon he knew that he was a sick man. Two men from the Battleford School met him there, with a democrat that he was expected to drive, while they drove the wagons loaded with supplies for the School. When they stopped on the trail at noon, John Matheson was too weak to drive any farther. The other men took the back seat out of the democrat, and made a bed for him there.

Neither of the young women would drive, and it was Gladys who took the lines in her small hands, to follow the loaded wagons at their slow pace for another three days. This was the trail by which the Barr Colonists had come five months before, and it had proved a hazardous way for many of their loaded wagons and carts.

The Eagle Hills were the hardest part of the trail, and the banks steep to the bridge that had been built over the creek in the wide ravine. As they came to the sharp descent to Eagle Creek, Gladys could hear her father's laboured breathing, and knew that he was barely conscious.

At the School, the doctor diagnosed pneumonia. Matheson insisted that Elizabeth was not to be told; and he made steady recovery, though it was another three weeks before he was strong enough to drive the rest of the way to Onion Lake.

In Winnipeg, Elizabeth was with her friends of Sunnyside and Cook's Creek days, John Grace's cousin Angus Henderson and his wife. Their home was on Spence Street, within walking distance of the Medical College on McDermott and Kate, though clinics were at the hospital, across a windy stretch of open prairie.

112

Just before Christmas Elizabeth learned that her baby was not well and the Hendersons urged her to bring him from Baie St. Paul to their home. Edward Matheson sent Mary Blackstar from the Battleford School to be the child's nurse. Every morning, at four o'clock, Elizabeth would begin her studies, and then attend to the baby's needs before she left him for the rest of the day with Mary.

She was the only woman in a class of more than twenty men; and she worked hard, finding the lectures and clinics stimulating after her limited practice and her isolation from all such contacts. It was her experience in the final examinations, however, that remained clearly in her memory.

She had to appear before Dr. Chown, the Dean, for her oral examination in surgery. The student who was leaving the room held the door open for her, and whispered as she passed, "Sprained knee." The advice was gratuitous and infuriating to Elizabeth.

Her honesty as an individual, and her pride as a woman were both affronted; her self-control had not returned when she heard Dr. Chown's voice, "This case has no previous history. What might it be?" There was the clue that she could follow, it seemed, to diagnose by the process of elimination, rather than give the only obvious answer. Still unsettled, she began the diagnosis aloud, "It might be tuberculosis. . . ." Dr. Chown stopped her. Impatiently, he directed her to other cases, each of which she was certain she diagnosed quickly and correctly.

The morning the list of graduates was posted, she was told that she had not been included. The men who were standing before the list moved aside in awkward silence to let her read it. Her name was not there. She had had time to compose herself, to decide what action she would take. "Where can I borrow a hood?" she asked. For a moment no one answered, and then one man said hesitantly, "Perhaps you should ask the Dean." The implication was clear.

With the same composure, however, she went to Dr. Chown's office. "I've come to ask if I may have a hood for graduation." His surprise was evident. "But you are not graduating." "You are mistaken, Dr. Chown. I am already a doctor, and I am convinced that I have actually passed every test here. You must know that my work has been satisfactory."

He stood up. "That's what others say. There's a faculty meeting now, and I'll bring the matter up. I can't say that I'm in favour of women in Medicine. This is a man's profession."

When he returned, his manner had changed. "You are right, *Dr.* Matheson." He stressed the title, even smiled as he gave her the hood he carried. He walked to the door with her, and they shook hands. Talk in the hallway fell into sudden silence; and only later that day did Elizabeth learn the outcome of her classmates' own hurried consultation. She carried their gift of roses when she went forward to receive her degree.

She registered with the College of Physicians and Surgeons in Manitoba, and when she returned to Onion Lake requested registration once again in the North-West Territories. The answer was unchanged. She would have to appear before members of the Council in Calgary.

John Matheson had had enough. "Call their bluff," he snapped, and wrote the cheque for her fifty-dollar fee. Her registration came by the next mail.

She would never know why the decision had been altered. Perhaps her registration in the College of Manitoba had been confirmed, and was so recognized. That would seem the most logical reason; and yet she held to her own explanation, for she was well aware of the discrimination against women in Medicine. She was certain that her registration came because of John Matheson's signature on the cheque. Until then, she was simply some unknown woman in the territory of the Saskatchewan who believed that she should be registered to practise Medicine without subscribing in every detail to the ruling of the College of Physicians and Surgeons.

During the winter that Elizabeth was in Winnipeg, there had been an outbreak of whooping-cough at the Mission, and Edith, the youngest of her little girls, not yet three years old, had developed it. Elizabeth sent what remedies might ease the coughing, but she was far away from them all, dependent upon mail that came only once in three weeks, and she had to wait anxiously for letters that brought more reassuring news.

When she returned to the Mission the child was still coughing, though summer did bring relief. Then winter came, and the coughing was renewed. Whooping-cough could be like that, Elizabeth reminded herself. Yet she found herself listening, troubled by doubt that would return over and over again in the years ahead. Did she only confuse the sound of Edith's cough with the memory of other tuberculous coughs? And if it was the same, what could she have done? There was to be no answer to that, for pneumonia suddenly developed, and late in December Edith died.

Elizabeth's grief was lost in John Grace's anguish for his child. And it tore her heart to witness this. Edith had turned to him in her mother's absence, exercising all the rights of the youngest, a golden-haired, loveable baby. And in dying, it was to him again that she had clung, her fingers having to be loosened from their grip on his.

For the rest of that winter, the routine work of the Mission continued, but

114

Wedding of Annie Phillips to James
Brown. Elizabeth (partly hidden) and
John are standing behind at the right.
Edith Matheson is the flower girl.

Manias and Ruth (1906).

St. Barnabas Mission on the Fort
Carlton-Ft. Edmonton trail (1906).

the buoyant spirit that had directed it was missing in John Grace. Only when springtime came did he rouse himself for the yearly trip to Edmonton.

The challenge of trading and buying, for a man of his nature, was a game of skill that brought its own release from other tensions. But there was more than just that release. There was healing in the journey itself, when English words and their association could be forgotten in the direct and simpler Cree; when encampments at night were in areas still empty of settlement, with the earth beneath and the stars of heaven above; and where the old trail and the mighty river recalled memories of his youth, and yet went on forever.

He came home to the Mission refreshed and reinvigorated, and in June, the happiness of his family was shared by the Mission and the Battleford School, when Edward Matheson and Eleanor Shepphird were married in the Mission Church of St. Barnabas. For Elizabeth and Eleanor, the name they now shared was the seal upon a long friendship; and the association between the Mathesons of Onion Lake and of Battleford became even stronger.

Elizabeth was with child once more, and she believed that if this should be another girl, it might seem to John Grace that Edith had been restored to them. Late in November, their seventh child was born, and they named her Ruth. Mrs. Slater attended the birth, but it was a difficult one, the labour prolonged through five days. When her exhaustion was passing, Elizabeth's interest as a doctor revived. She asked Mrs. Slater for the after-birth, to examine it, but she was too late. It had been burned; and the question as to whether this could have been to some degree a twin-birth had to go unanswered.

Twenty-Three

In 1905, there were sixty-six children in the school, only sixteen of them Treaty Indians. The staff had increased, and the work of the Mission was coming to its full development, the buildings evidence of its scope and diversity.

The church had been rebuilt at last, on a good foundation; and the three-storey frame school-house had been in use for more than a year. Since 1904, the original school had been gone, its logs taken down and numbered carefully, to be freighted to Lloydminster by Indians, who helped the colonists build their own church, St. John's Minster, from these logs.

On the Mission grounds, there were adequate storehouses, and a log cottage for the men employed in outside work. As well, there was the two-storey log structure that John Matheson planned to raise to three, converting the building into a hospital for Elizabeth, as a memorial to their little girl.

To travellers along that western trail, the Mission House appeared as a large rambling home, with verandah, balcony, cupola, and bay windows that overlooked Elizabeth's garden. Expanded as it was by additions and alterations to the original four-roomed house, its plan was simply one of convenience, adapted to each year's growth, and the finances of the builder.

The rooms varied in size and in number according to purpose. The two largest were the children's dining-room and the girls' dormitory. As well as the outside stairway to the balcony, there were four entrances, which were never locked—the south door into the front hallway and sitting-room, the one least used, the others leading to working areas. On the west side between Elizabeth's dispensary and her husband's office was the ''Indian room'' with its outer door providing ready access to all who sought either John Matheson or the doctor.

In name, this was the Anglican Mission, but John Grace was a trader, builder, and rancher too, and he was called upon in any of these capacities, or simply as a friend. Elizabeth, as a doctor, received all who came for her attention, and visited any of the homes on the Reserves in the Mission charge, or in the Metis settlements. Homesteads north of the river were not yet surveyed, and that part of her practice among white settlers was only beginning. Through her work, and through John Grace's wide contacts and friendship, she came to know every family in the whole area.

The Reserve on which the Mission was located had been surveyed in 1878, and named for Chief Sekaskooch, who had signed the Treaty at Fort Pitt in 1876. During the disturbed weeks of 1885 that preceded and followed the massacre at Frog Lake, he had kept his Band withdrawn in the northern bush. When the Alberta Field Force reached Fort Pitt, and was moving on to Frenchman's Butte and its encounter with Big Bear's warriors, two of Major Steele's scouts came upon the encampment of Sekaskooch's Band. The old Chief was sitting in the doorway of his tent, smoking his pipe, when they shot him; and they shot his eldest son as he was driving the horses in from their pasture to the camp.

The younger son was scarcely out of boyhood, but he went then, with others of the Band, to join Big Bear, though it was only for the retreat to Loon Lake, and surrender. Still, he had been a rebel, and for years was denied the right to become Chief himself, however highly the others of the Band might regard him. When he took a Christian name in baptism, he added the distinctive surname that he regarded his by right, becoming Robert Chief.

His wife was a grand-daughter of Big Bear; one of her sisters, the wife of Ka-nē-pa-tā-tāo, chief dancer of that fiercely resistant band of Plains Cree; and another, the youngest, married to Andrew Sinclair, who had been one of the boys who had come of his own accord to stay at the Mission school in that first winter of 1892. All three were proud and passionate women.

After the celebrations of Christmas and New Year's Day 1906 the three men and their families left the Reserve to trap in the northern bush.

Early one Sunday morning, not two weeks later, Andrew came to the Mission to report that they had brought back with them from their hunting camp, the bodies of two of Robert Chief's children; and Elizabeth, upon questioning him, was reasonably certain that diphtheria had been the cause of their deaths.

She went with her husband to the one-roomed house, three miles from the Mission. As they approached they could hear the wailing of the women; and found the house filled with men, women and children. John Matheson's coming was accepted, since they had sent for him, and Robert Chief came forward with Andrew and Ka-nē-pa-tā-tāo to speak to him; but Elizabeth knew at once that her presence as doctor was resented by their wives as an intrusion upon their grief. They opposed her with unyielding silence.

The bodies of the three children lay in a corner of the room. She had to insist upon examining them; and it was only with her husband's patient cooperation that she was able to draw from some of those present in the room a reluctant description of the onset and course of the fatal illness. It was definitely diphtheria.

Late in the afternoon, when the funeral at the church was over, she came back to the house, and again John Grace was with her to help if possible. Her questions fell into the same resisting silence; the children were snatched from her, or hid of their own accord; she could not examine them, and to inoculate was out of the question.

Once more she had to retreat before hostile resistance, but she had gained one point. They would have to accept quarantine, though they could choose the place. They chose a house where there had been no death, and one that was farther than Robert Chief's from this persistent white woman. It was Ka-nē-pa-tā-tāo's, a full six miles from the Mission. Elizabeth and John Grace accompanied the three families there, made certain of their needs, and notified the Agent, that he might send rations for nineteen men, women and

118

children. The other mourners were permitted to disperse to their homes.

In spite of the resistance she had encountered, Elizabeth's anxiety drew her every day to the house, but without effect. On Friday, she noticed that Andrew Sinclair's little girl was not well, and she asked to examine her. The mother turned upon her then in open fury, crying out in Cree, "It is only out of a black heart that you come to torture us in our grief." Elizabeth's patience snapped. In angry Cree, she stormed at them all, "I will not come back again unless you send for me," and left the house.

All that night, and all the next day, snow fell. And it was bitterly cold. It would have been difficult to drive those miles of unbroken trail in any case, but it was still anger that restrained Elizabeth, and not until Saturday night did this change to remorse.

It was too dark then to find her way. The trail was quite obscured, the mercury falling steadily. She told her driver that he must have the team and sleigh ready for her at the first light, and she waited anxiously for the night to pass. In the morning, it was forty-four degrees below zero. She recorded that reading for the meteorogical department in Ottawa in the bitter grey dawn, just before she began her drive across the Reserve.

A mile from the Mission, her driver saw another sleigh approaching. The Indian who was driving it pulled his team from the road into the deep snow to let them pass, and in the growing light she recognized Andrew. Swift anger surged again. This was how he kept quarantine. At her sudden exclamation, her driver pulled the team to a sharp halt. "What are you doing here?" she snapped at Sinclair. His answering voice was heavy with grief, scarcely audible. "Don't say anything now," he begged. "Drive as fast as you can. My little girl is very sick."

She was dying. Elizabeth adminstered antitoxin, yet knew that the child could not live. She asked to examine the other children. In hushed silence, the women brought their children to her one after another for inoculation. One small boy struggled against his mother's restraining arms and began to cry. Robert Chief took down a brace and bit from the wall, and stepped towards him. "Let the doctor put her medicine into you," he ordered, "or I'll bore a hole right through you with this." The startled child looked from his uncle's grim face to the grave faces about him, and submitted to the needle without a sound.

When Elizabeth returned in the afternoon, the little girl had died. The next day, she was called to another house, where a child was sick. The mother had been a mourner for Robert's children, and had been given a shawl in which one of them had been wrapped. Her own child, though inoculated, did not survive, dying two weeks later of paralysis of the heart muscles. The shawl had to be traced to a third house, and thoroughly disinfected. Three more cases of diphtheria developed, but all of these were mild.

For weeks, Elizabeth drove those miles each day, fulfilling her duty, yet alert to her responsibility for all the children at the Mission too, and these included her own nursing infant of two months. Standing by her sleigh, outside each house that she visited, she would change from her outer garments to a surgical cap and gown for the care of the sick; and in all those weeks, the temperature varied by only a few degrees from the reading that she had recorded in the first week.

School-children (1907)—with Miss Kemp and Miss McMullen.

Her practice was now established, and Indians came almost daily to her dispensary for treatment. Often, because of the conditions and circumstances of their lives and of the times, there could be only alleviation of their distress. For Blind Anne (blindness was common, either from cataracts that were the affliction of the aged, or from the prevalence of trachoma) the tonic that Elizabeth mixed contained some strychnine, and it was to last two weeks, as she carefully explained. It was finished in two days, and Blind Anne seemed quite unaffected by any overdose when she came back for more of the fine medicine. The second bottle contained no strychnine, however, and she asked for no more, the medicine having lost its potency for her.

A man called Ahkinew came to Elizabeth with a cough which she knew was tuberculous. To ease it a little, she gave him a quart bottle filled with an emulsion of whisky and cod-liver oil. He was to shake it well before taking; and she gave a vigorous demonstration. Then, watching with what tender care he received and carried the bottle, she knew that his one concern would be to allow the emulsion to settle. For once, she could let him have that happy satisfaction. When he returned to the dispensary, he used every art of Indian oratory to praise the wondrous medicine. Only let him have it in two bottles, that he might mix it with more care. It was a disillusioned old man who trudged homewards. He had found that the medicine-woman could forget all her Cree and understand not a sign, for she gave him some tea and tobacco, but no medicine at all.

The dispensary was only part of her work, the easier part. She went on house calls to attend many of her patients; and these calls took her as far as Frog Lake, or farther still to Island Lake, with its most difficult trail. She would visit several homes and be away from her own for days at a time; but members of the staff were competent, and her widowed mother came to live at the Mission to care for her younger grandchildren.

Twenty-Four

Settlement north of the river had to wait upon completion of surveys, but to the south, development was rapid in the wake of the Barr Colonists. The Canadian Northern Railway had been extended on to Edmonton, with passenger service in operation to Lloydminster by November 1905.

More than twenty years before, the choice of the southern route for the Canadian Pacific had moved the seat of government for the Territories from Battleford to Regina. Speculators still profited or lost all along the right of way; and at Battleford their greed was to ruin the little town when the Canadian Northern built its bridge miles to the east, and then established North Battleford across the Saskatchewan from the old town.

Lloydminster flourished. It had three hotels, stores, a bank, even its own newspaper. Villages and hamlets sprang up along the line of the railroad; cable-ferries were soon operating on the river, and mail came twice a week to Onion Lake.

All these changes had their effect upon the Mission, and John Grace adapted to them; but he continued still to trade chiefly at Edmonton, and to bring his goods down the river by scow. Railroads and settlement might change the face of the whole country, but since 1869, when he had first come to the Saskatchewan, and years before the needs of the Mission were his compelling force, John Grace had pitted his strength and ingenuity against the river; and for him the Saskatchewan and the old Fort Carlton-Fort Edmonton trail would remain a challenge so long as his strength should last.

His business ventures, and Elizabeth's growing practice, both had their impact upon the Mission, extending its activities well beyond any church-centred role.

To their children, that enterprising, striving life, with the frequent absence of one parent or the other, seemed the normal way. In their earliest years, the Mission was their whole world; later, when each in turn was sent away to school, returning for holidays, the memories of childhood summers were strengthened.

All winter long there was sleighing on the hills and skating on the frozen sloughs. The children experienced the joyous interlude of Christmas, with carols, a towering spruce in the school-room, a gift for every child; they shared in the celebrations of New Year, instituted by French and Scottish fur-traders, whose regale for the Indians was more potent than the Mission's tea and currant scones.

But it was when the children heard the honking of the wild geese, saw those V-shaped squadrons winging from the south, that they came to vigorous life again. The hills would be wondrous with the blue of crocuses;

John and Elizabeth Matheson with their family (1906).
From left to right: Letitia, Grace, Selkirk, Gladys, and Riema. The baby is Ruth.

the meadow-larks at every fence corner would be singing lustily, "We-fed-the-Is-rae-lites", and the children, brimming with an equal force of spring, would mimic them, carolling back in Cree "Bring-me-the-axe", or stoutly insisting in English, "You never did. The Bible says God sent quails."

Spring could impel the Indian children to escape any restraint; and the others would scarcely have been the children of John Grace and Elizabeth without the urge to seek adventure. Rosalie's daughters were their constant companions. Each spring there were the hills to climb, the creek to wade, marsh marigolds to gather by the armful. They would wander where the muskeg spread, sunlight filtering though spruce boughs, to find fringed gentian and yellow lady's slipper. Or they would visit the camps that summer brought to the vicinity of the Mission, welcomed as "grandchildren" into sun-warmed tents and teepees that smelled of woodsmoke and tanned leather and kinne-kinnick tobacco, where Nocum (Grandmother) sat, smoking her pipe, small lined face and wizened hands relaxed—Old Georgina (Cho-chena) telling stories of her own childhood in the long-ago days of warfare with the Blackfoot.

And all around the fields and pastures of the Mission were fences of strong poplar poles, six and eight rails high, to climb constantly, scorning the stiles and gates. During long summer days, the children would follow one another in a kind of solemn pilgrimage, balancing barefoot on the topmost rail, arms outstretched, determined to walk around one side at least of the enclosure, but seldom succeeding, always lured by the unattainable, skinning elbows and shins, risking broken bones.

Riema did succeed in walking the four sides of one square, but it was a relatively small one, and the logs of spruce and pine were large. Besides, she had been dared to do it, and though she was the mildest and most gentle little girl, she could not refuse. It was just that she had to climb a long ladder to get there; for these logs were two storeys up, the unfinished structure of what would be in time her mother's hospital.

She chose the noon-hour to accomplish the feat, when the Mission yard was empty of all except her necessary witnesses. But someone ran for her father when it was already too late to stop her. He stood beside Elizabeth, and watched. Neither of them spoke, and they stayed out of sight, though Riema was intent only upon the exact placing of each bare foot in turn, and her balance.

It was when she had returned to the starting point and was climbing down the ladder, that her father walked across the yard. "Well done, N'tanis," he called encouragingly; and then, when her feet were firmly upon the ground, "But don't let me ever catch you at that again."

Some years later, when her father was not at home, Grace met with a serious accident. It began with a broody hen that had lost all interest in a setting of eggs; and Grace was determined it should return to duty. She had chased it across the yard, and into the shed where sleighs and cutters were stored, steel runners up. The hen flew into the rafters above, round poles from which harness could hang. Grace pulled herself up and edged her way cautiously towards the cackling bird; but the pole turned and the child was flung backwards onto one of the runners below, to lie there, limp as a rag doll, without sound or movement.

One of the other children ran for Elizabeth, and Grace was carried carefully to the Mission; but she remained unconscious, and the red welt across her spine could have meant a crippling or fatal injury.

John Grace had been in Saskatoon, and was driving to Lloydminster, where he was expected that day. Elizabeth telegraphed the hotel; midnight passed, and the child regained consciousness, was able to move her limbs freely, without evidence of injury.

It was not yet morning when her father returned, and hours later when Elizabeth remarked on how quickly he had responded to her telegram. He took her to the pasture, let down a bar of the gate, and whistled, rattling a pail of oats. Horses grazing at the far end lifted their heads and trotted eagerly towards them, one moving swiftly ahead with the graceful rocking gait of a pacer. "See that. Annie Rooney, she's registered. And she's yours."

Grace Matheson (*c.* 1904).

The mare nuzzled the oats, and Elizabeth stroked her outstretched neck. Dark bay—like Abdul in India—and the word for "brown" in Hindustani she remembered was "Malin". That would be her name; it had a sound to it that seemed to suit her.

He had bought the mare in Saskatoon, enchanted by her speed and pace; and had driven her by easy stages to Lloydminster, arriving late in the evening. When the telegram reached him, he had hurried to the livery barn, harnessed her again to the light buggy and driven through the sleeping town to the river, more than twenty miles to Hewitt's landing. The ferryman was asleep, and Matheson had not stayed to waken him. He had left the rowboat on the south bank and taken the ferry across himself, propelling the heavy craft out until the current caught it, and at cable-length carried it across to the other bank. And even with that delay, the mare had made the trip of thirty-five miles, added to the forty-five miles of her day-time journey, in less than four hours.

Twenty-Five

However much Elizabeth trusted her husband's judgment in all these matters, she stood firm on the one thing that concerned her more deeply than any other—the education of their daughters.

He had found her own training of inestimable value to them both, and had insisted that she carry it to completion at any cost to herself; yet for his daughters, he would have dismissed higher education as of no real importance had she not insisted.

While they were still children, some of his reluctance to consider their education seriously was because they had to leave the Mission to continue it beyond the most elementary level, and he found it hard to part with them. When they were older he could plead their indispensibility in the work of the Mission. How could higher education be of more value to a girl than the training that his daughters had in the work of the Mission? Elizabeth had to yield at times, but only to urge again and again that he give his girls more opportunity.

In 1903, he had brought Gladys most willingly back with him from Winnipeg; and it was late in the school year of 1905-06, when she was thirteen, before she was sent away again, and then only to Battleford, where she stayed with the Scotts. Riema and Letitia went at the same time, to live with the Mathesons in the principal's residence at the Industrial School.

Together, the three attended the town school, Gladys and Riema in the senior class, Letitia in the junior.

In the fall, they returned to Battleford, but John Grace had been persuaded finally that Gladys should go to a girls' school in the east. Through the work of the Mission, both he and Elizabeth had made friends in almost every city of Canada, and they were advised to send their daughter to a school in Ottawa, operated by the Kilburn Sisters, who had shown a kindly interest for years in the work of missions in the Diocese of Saskatchewan.

John Grace decided to travel with her, not only to make certain that Gladys would be happy there, but to use the opportunity to discuss the problems of his own school with officials of the Department of Indian Affairs.

They left the Mission on the 28th of January, and reached Ottawa on February 15. They had stopped in Winnipeg for a three-day visit. There were delays all along the way, even in Lloydminster, where Gladys visited with H. B. Hall's family until the train from Edmonton finally arrived on February 2.

She recorded some of her impressions of that trip, and its uncertainties, in a notebook that had been given to her as a parting gift:

> Feb. 2. Left Halls' at 6.30 as we heard the train was due. We had to wait until a quarter to nine, and we left at nine-thirty. I had had no supper, and Papa was in the middle of his at Bruce's Hotel when he had to come for me. We ran nearly all the way to the station, and then had to wait for nearly three hours.
>
> Feb. 3. Radisson: We have been stuck for about seven hours here. There is a train from the east stuck in the snow and that is why we cannot go on.
>
> Feb. 4. Humboldt: We got here at twenty minutes to three in the afternoon, and it is now five minutes after nine the next morning. There is no water, and the cars are getting cold as there is no fire either. They had to put the engines in the round-house. We were all sent to the Windsor Hotel, and the C. N. R. will pay our expenses.
>
> We left Humboldt on the 5th at a quarter to five in the morning. We heard on the 4th that the train was leaving at midnight, and we sat up all night playing Flinch, and at two in the morning we left the hotel, and had to sit on the train until a quarter to five. We made a lot of friends in Humboldt. The conductor took Mrs. Clines, Miss Walker and myself to the hotel, and helped us carry

our suitcases. He got us a room with two beds. The hotel was clean, but the waitresses, especially one, seemed very gloomy. I shall never forget my journey to Ottawa, and my halt at Humboldt.
Feb. 6. Wadena: Last night, the Rev. James Taylor of Emmanuel College, and myself sang Cree hymns in the car.

In Ottawa, the headmistress introduced her to the other girls at supper with the unexpected request: "Gladys Matheson has come from an Indian Mission in Saskatchewan. We shall ask her for the blessing in Cree." Heads were bowed, and Gladys hesitated for only a moment. When she had finished her words in Cree, there was a general sigh, and the headmistress said, "That is a long blessing." "Oh, that wasn't a blessing. I don't know any in Cree. That was just the Gloria. I know the Lord's Prayer by heart too, and that is really long."

John Grace repeated the story to Elizabeth. Their lively daughter was ready to meet any situation it seemed, and her engaging charm would win her friends.

Having let Gladys go, John Grace was prepared to consider sending another of the girls away, though not to Ottawa. Dunham Ladies' College, just outside Montreal, was the next choice; and it was Letitia who went there late in October, travelling with Archdeacon J. A. Mackay who was on his way to England.

It had been agreed that Riema should stay with her aunt and uncle at the principal's residence at the Battleford School. She would be happier there, for she was a quiet, dreaming girl, without the easy assurance of her older sister, or of Letitia who was only eleven.

For two years, their Aunt Eleanor had been coaching them in proper behaviour, stressing the superior manners and civilization of the east, and of Toronto in particular. In Montreal, on the night that she arrived, Letitia regarded that vaunted civilization with amazement, seeing other children in outlandish garb, begging from door to door. No one at Onion Lake would dream of behaving like that. It was her first experience with Hallowe'en.

Letitia adjusted to school life as readily as Gladys had. She spent the summer on a farm in the Eastern Townships, while Gladys went to the Gatineau with Judge and Mrs. Armstrong. In September, the two sisters were together at Dunham for a final year before returning to the Mission in July 1909.

At the Mission, Elizabeth's log hospital had been completed in the summer of 1908, when a skilled workman came from the Barr Colony to lathe and plaster the interior properly. It had an operating room and four wards on the upper floors, a verandah and balcony, and an outside stairway to the second floor. The lower floor continued to serve as laundry room and carpentry shop.

The hospital was never in steady use, and members of staff could usually help the doctor, though in epidemics a trained nurse was called in from Winnipeg and would stay for several months. There were three such epidemics. The first one was measles, a most serious disease among the Indians who had no immunity to it.

For an Indian admitted to the hospital the government allowed a grant of one dollar per day. There was always a fear of being separated from the family, however. Separation could be difficult for white settlers too, the charge of one dollar per day practically prohibitive. Because of this, even when her practice extended into the growing settlements, Elizabeth would continue to attend nearly all her patients in their own homes. The hospital would serve only rarely for obstetrics, or for non-epidemic sicknesses. Its chief function would be for minor surgery and accident cases.

It was the dispensary at the Mission which was used more often. In the summer of 1908, when the hospital was being built, one of the workmen had an accident that required the doctor's attention. He had been squaring a log on the outer wall, and had thrown his adze to the ground before he jumped down, landing on the upright blade. The wound was deep, but it was clean and healed readily.

Only a few days before that accident, Ka-ta-mis-ka-wat (He who shakes hands) had persuaded Elizabeth to remove an enlarged gland from the back of his neck. It was as big as an orange, but easily removed, and Elizabeth placed it in a basin while she closed the incision. Ka-ta-mis-ka-wat's wife was with him in the dispensary, and the strange object fascinated her. Elizabeth opened the sac and showed her the rice-like contents. A mouse's nest, the woman decided immediately, and it seemed a fair enough conclusion.

When either Ka-ta-mis-ka-wat or the workman appeared for a dressing, one of the children would run breathlessly for the doctor. "Here's your man with the neck." "It's your man with the foot, Mamma."

There were many obstetrical cases, though often Elizabeth was not called until the delivery proved difficult. Her own confinement that summer went smoothly, with Mrs. Slater's cheerful assistance again. This was another daughter, her seventh. They named her Kathleen to please her Irish Godmother, a member of staff, and they added the name Agnes, for the noted writer Agnes Laut, who had visited the Mission a few days before the child's birth.

John Matheson at Onion Lake, with Peter Thunder's son (Big Bear's grandson) and Selkirk Matheson.

Left: the Mission Hospital.
Right: the log cottage for workmen at the Mission.

Agnes Laut was widely known then as a newspaper woman, biographer and historian. Her history of the Hudson's Bay Company had just been completed, and she was making a journey by canoe down the Saskatchewan River from Edmonton to Grand Rapids. Gertrude Simpson, the grand-niece of Sir George, was with her, and they were accompanied by a man.

It was Agnes Laut's intention to visit all the Hudson's Bay Company posts along the Saskatchewan, to gather material for further articles. From the site of Fort Pitt, she was brought to the post at Onion Lake, though with some reluctance, for her driver knew that conditions there, after a night of heavy drinking, were not favourable for such visitors. One glimpse satisfied the writer, and she was thankful to be taken to the Mission instead.

Her coming was quite unexpected, but so too was her experience in meeting John Matheson, though she had known his cousin in Winnipeg, and had been the Archbishop's secretary briefly. She stayed on for another day, completely charmed by John Grace. His stories gave her material for articles in several periodicals, and she was to draw upon her impressions of him for a character in one of her novels.

Twenty-Six

In the summer of 1909, the family were all together at the Mission, the three older girls home from school. The change in Gladys and Letitia after their long absence was the more surprising to their parents, for Riema had come home from Battleford for other holidays, and they had seen her at frequent intervals. All three had emerged from that somewhat amorphous state of childhood that may be imposed in a large family; and they could no longer be grouped simply as "the children".

Gladys was almost seventeen, a most captivating young creature, with verve to which the school's training had lent a slight air of elegance but which no rules or precepts could possibly confine within a set pattern of behaviour.

That her return from school should coincide with the opening of settlement north of the river had an enlivening effect at the Mission. Lonely homesteaders, surveyors, Hudson's Bay Company clerks and Mounted Police revealed surprising interest in the day-to-day activities; and on Sunday, at the evening service in English, young tenors and baritones made the hills truly resound.

Gladys was the lively centre of it all, for she loved people and they were all her friends, settlers and Indians alike. It was expected that she would stay now to help in the work of the Mission, and she gave herself with willing spirit, until her father would agree to let her go to begin her training as a nurse.

To Riema, the principal's residence at the Battleford School had been home for almost four years, and her affection would remain divided. While her sisters were away, she had shared in the happiness that the birth of a son had brought to Edward and Eleanor Matheson; and then in the anguish of his death from whooping-cough before he was a year old.

Grief for her only child might have closed Eleanor Matheson's heart then against all the small Mathesons who abounded and thrived at the Mission, and against the woman who could so naturally and often bear children. But it was not so. The friendship between herself and Elizabeth only deepened into the love of sisters, and the children might have belonged to them equally. Riema and Letitia in particular would always be like daughters to Eleanor Matheson; and they in turn had loved her from their first acquaintance.

For Letitia, her aunt's understanding and affection provided what she most needed. The relationship between herself and her mother never quite overcame the shock it had sustained, both in the sudden separation when she was a baby, and then in her hurried and impatient return to the family. The lack of warmth between them may have stemmed from a certain similarity between mother and daughter, in their more reserved natures, where the others could be responsive and outgoing.

At Dunham, Letitia's lovely voice had been recognized, and she began her first tentative lessons, opening the world of music to her. She had been able to establish her own identity apart from her sisters. Then Gladys came to join her at Dunham. Whereas it would never have been in Riema's nature to dispute the sway of their older sister, Letitia made it evident that she would not yield again, that she was an individual in her own right. After her return to Saskatchewan, resistance would be her attitude throughout adolescence towards family and teachers alike, with the exception of one person, her Aunt Eleanor.

The gracious serenity of the home at Battleford would seem to the girl as far removed from the hurly-burly of life at the Mission, as Eleanor Matheson's unruffled calm was from Elizabeth's quick impatience, or Eleanor's careful regard for appearance and dress from Elizabeth's apparent disregard. If it sometimes appeared that Elizabeth had slept in her clothes, that was precisely what her calls at crowded lonely shacks, her days upon the trail did compel. All her skill as a dressmaker, her flair for style, went into making the clothes that her daughters required—for schools that stressed the gentle conventions and manners their Aunt Eleanor represented.

131

And yet, at the Mission, it was Elizabeth's warm expressive reading that made books come alive for her children; it was she who made certain there was a tennis court where her growing girls could learn to play the game that she had loved to play herself in India; it was she who bought the piano for the sitting-room, that Letitia's voice might fill the Mission House with song; and it was she above all who continued to insist that however much was required of the girls in the work of the Mission, they should still be given the opportunity for further training and education.

St. Alban's Ladies' College in Prince Albert helped make this possible. It was established in 1909, by the Right Reverend Jervois Arthur Newnham and Mrs. Newnham who came to the Diocese in 1904. There were five daughters in their own family, and it was natural that they should be concerned about the education of girls.

Arabella Florence Ryan was headmistress until 1915, and was succeeded then by Janet Virtue, both able women who usually recruited their teachers from the British Isles and developed the school programme according to the standards of other girls' schools in England and eastern Canada.

Until 1918, as long as there were Newnhams at St. Alban's, there was also at least one of "those wild Mathesons from the bush." Riema and Letitia went in September 1909. Riema endured Miss Ryan's out-spoken criticism of Canadian ways, her unfeeling sarcasm, for only one school-year. Riema was too gentle, too easily imposed upon, and the following year her Aunt Eleanor took her back to her Battleford home. Grace was sent to St. Alban's in her place. Under Miss Dowding and Eileen Fitzgerald, who had come from the Abbey Theatre in Dublin, Grace developed her own talents in art, drama, and in elocution—which was much in vogue at that time. Her unpredictable ways might continue to exasperate others, but to these mistresses she was often a delight.

At the Mission, Gladys applied herself with lively energy wherever she was needed, assistant to her mother, to the school-teacher and matrons, and partner with Manias in some of the general work and responsibility for the three small children of the family. Kathleen had been born while Gladys was away at school, and neither Selkirk nor Ruth had any earlier memory of her before she returned with all the freshness and gaiety of someone from another world.

"She's a good girl," Elizabeth remarked, with characteristic understatement, and John Grace agreed heartily, and then added, "But she'll have a long way to go before she's a patch on her mother."

Twenty-Seven

Early in September 1910, Elizabeth's last child was born, a boy whom they named John Richard for his father, though John Grace spoke of him as "my little Benjamin, the son of my old age." With Mrs. Slater in attendance, the birth was normal, but the child was not as robust as Elizabeth's earlier ones. Then she recognized that she was developing puerperal fever, and sent to Lloydminster for Dr. Hill. As she recovered her health, the boy too gained strength. But, at four months, meningeal croup ended his brief life.

From September until Easter, Letitia was kept from school to relieve Gladys of some of her duties so that she could help and comfort their mother. Elizabeth was more concerned for her daughters; and with the opening of the spring term, Letitia was back at St. Alban's, and Gladys in training at a Prince Albert hospital. Six months later, Gladys returned to the Mission, on the advice of her aunt.

Eleanor Matheson was then diocesan president of the Woman's Auxiliary to the Missionary Society. Through that work she had many friends and a closer contact with the general activity of the whole area than Elizabeth had in her isolated situation. When Eleanor was told that the girls in training at Prince Albert were more exploited as cheap labour than trained as nurses, she visited the hospital, and was able to confirm this in the light of her own earlier training in Toronto. Gladys could learn as much with her mother, until she could enter a recognized training school.

In the meantime, at the Mission again, she was the leader of a most engaging trio, for Riema at seventeen had completed her school days in Battleford, and Manias at the same age was already a competent staff member.

When an epidemic of typhoid fever filled the hospital with serious cases, all three girls were enlisted under a trained nurse from Winnipeg. There were no deaths. However the disinfectant that was used then for all sanitation purposes, even for the washing of walls and floors, was bichloride of mercury. And the girls were saturated with it. The effects wore off, though extreme sensitivity to even the mildest solution was to continue for a time.

For most medical services, the dispensary remained the centre. On the day that Billie Patenaude came for help, the doctor was absent. It was Gladys who heard him shouting and cursing wildly. He was only partly sober from a drunken fight that had left him with a bloody hand, one finger bitten

133

to the bone. Gladys met him at the door of the dispensary. "Stop that, or I'll not let you in. None of that swearing if you want my help." Taken aback, he mumbled, "A'ri, Gla's, a'ri," and sat quietly in the dispensary while she brought a kettle of steaming water from the kitchen. She poured some of it into a basin to cool while she unlocked a cupboard door for the carbolic disinfectant, and added that. Then she plunged his hand into the basin, and he cursed most effectively again. She jerked the basin away. "You promised me," she shouted at him above the uproar. "But that water's too god-damned hot," he roared back; and then meekly put his hand in again. The wound did heal, and his finger was saved.

Against blood-poisoning, hot water and fomentations were still the principal weapons; and if Gladys's whole-hearted use of them was to ensure her remembrance with many patients, it was her understanding warmth that won their friendship—a friendship that was to endure for sixty years in the case of Charlie and Josephine Parenteau.

In 1901, Charlie had been Elizabeth's first patient with smallpox. At the close of 1911, when he and Josephine had been married only four days, it was blood-poisoning of his hand and arm that brought him to the doctor, to have the swelling lanced and hot fomentations applied every twenty minutes.

Gladys was the nurse, and the treatment went on during the day and far into New Year's Eve, long after the Watch-night service had ended and the Mission was asleep. There were wood-burning stoves in every room, but the fires had to be guarded most carefully, and well banked at night. The fire in the kitchen range was the only one kept hot enough to boil water. A bed was made on the floor for Charlie. Josephine sat huddled and sick at heart, just out of the way, her eyes clouded with tears for Charlie's distress.

When Gladys was certain that the inflammation had yielded, she whispered to the girl, "You get in there beside Charlie. You'll both feel better then. I'll come back again before anyone else is stirring."

She and Josephine had known one another since childhood, when Josephine and her sister had been little girls in the Mission school. They were the daughters of Ethel Quinney, who had been married in the Roman Catholic Church to an Irishman, William Dillon, before the Mathesons came to Onion Lake.

In 1898, John Matheson had written to Ottawa: "I have for some time past kept these children at my own expense. Their mother is a Treaty Indian, and she lives with her parents on this Reserve. Her husband has deserted her for more than a year and is hardly likely ever to return. Why should these poor children be refused a privilege (the grant for schooling) that is accorded to the illegitimate because their mother had the misfortune to be lawfully married to a scamp?''

Obtaining the grant had changed the whole situation, however, for the girls were nominally Roman Catholic, and would have to be enrolled in that school. And Dillon did return to make certain of that, though the welfare of his children's souls or of their bodies had been a matter of indifference to him until then.

His stay on the Reserve was brief, but Elizabeth would never forget the day that he came to the Mission, seeking to justify his action in withdrawing the girls. John Grace had finished digging an outside entrance to the cellar, and was shoring it with two-by-fours when Dillon walked around a corner of the house to stand just above the cellar-way, his back to the open window at which Elizabeth was sewing. Dillon had not noticed her, and she remained silent.

On his part, John Grace barely acknowledged Dillon's greeting before he turned again to his work, making no response when the Irishman launched into a recitation of all the concern that he felt for his daughters' welfare, and particularly for their religious training.

The silence infuriated Dillon, and his voice grew louder and louder. Then he noticed a short length of two-by-four lumber at his feet and, with a sudden movement, he lifted it and swung it full at John Grace's down-bent head. Elizabeth screamed, and the unexpected cry startled Dillon and deflected his aim; John Grace dodged, flinging up his arm to catch the blow; and Dillon dropped the scantling and ran.

Matheson leaped from the cellar-way, and was gaining steadily as they raced across the yard. At a mud-puddle near the gate, he tripped Dillon and rubbed his face in the mud before throwing him bodily out the gateway.

There was some satisfaction in that, but it did not help the girls much. The whole incident did have one effect though. The Mathesons subsequently decided to adopt Rosalie's children legally, so that no errant father might claim them whenever it suited his purpose.

Twenty-Eight

There were two other children, a boy and a girl, who were in the school for years, and for whom—in particular for Ellen—the Mathesons felt a special concern. She was one of the loveliest of girls and a tender relationship developed between Elizabeth and her.

When Ellen was about sixteen, Elizabeth found her crying one day, and took her into her arms. "Tell me what's wrong." But Ellen could only sob, "It's my mother. It's always my mother. I know that some day I'll be like that too." There was no balm in Gilead could ease that pain, no healing in any of the training that Elizabeth had known. Ellen's mother was insane.

Oo-ni-ka-moos had once been lovely herself; her name "The Singer" indicated only one of the talents she had possessed. She had become insane, Elizabeth was told, after the birth and death of her first child. She had been at Thunderchild's Reserve then, sixty miles from Onion Lake and her own people; and she had refused to believe that the child was dead, had continued to cradle it in her arms, and was making her desolate way on foot back to Onion Lake, when the Police were notified and overtook her.

That had been before the Mathesons had known her. John Grace could usually soothe her wild outbursts with his easy Cree and a pipeful of tobacco; but Elizabeth had aroused her distrust, and could never break the barrier between them.

It had happened quite without intention, in Elizabeth's first year at the Mission, before she understood Cree. John Grace had been absent that day, and Elizabeth was baking bread while she served their noon meal to two white men who were helping with the building. Oo-ni-ka-moos was in the kitchen, and she heard the light talk in English, and Elizabeth's laughter. To the Indian woman, this was sheer wantonness, betrayal of a trusting husband; and there was only one way she could think of avenging him. She would burn that precious bread. She began to push stick after stick of wood into the fire-box; and when Elizabeth tried to prevent her, she struck her angrily about the head and shoulders with a heavy stick, until the men managed to restrain the crazed woman.

That resentment never quite died, though when her son and daughter were admitted to the school, Oo-ni-ka-moos camped for most of each year just outside the Mission grounds, to be near them.

Her visits to the Mission were frequent, and usually someone watched carefully, though she never harmed anyone again. Then, one Sunday morning, just before the Cree service began, one of Elizabeth's patients returned a bottle of belladonna liniment that she had been given for her own use. In the hurried departure for the church, it was placed on a high shelf in the kitchen, and Elizabeth was told about it when the service ended. She went to get it and found that the bottle contained only coloured water. Someone then recalled that Oo-ni-ka-moos had been present when the liniment was returned; and Elizabeth hurried to her camp with a strong emetic.

Oo-ni-ka-moos was lying on the ground of her tent, limp from the poison.

Her sister, Martha Painter, was with her, and she watched Elizabeth lift the lolling head and force some of the emetic into her mouth. Unexpectedly Oo-ni-ka-moos spat it into Elizabeth's face. Elizabeth sprang away in disgust, and then pushed the bottle with the remaining emetic into Martha's hands. "You make her take it, or she'll die. It's no use me trying." She left the tent, and Martha's method was evidently more compelling, or else her sister no longer had strength to resist, for the emetic was successful. Oo-ni-ka-moos returned to the hopeless life she had tried unwittingly to end.

In Granny Wolf's case, there was no haunting discouragement. The torment lay chiefly in being deprived of tobacco; and in this case she was surrounded by family. It was her son who rode at a gallop to the Mission to report the strange sickness that had come upon his mother without warning. She would not tell them what distressed her, only sit there, with queer moaning sounds, her face distorted, her mouth gaping. Everyone was frightened, and the doctor must come quickly.

Elizabeth reached the house and found it filled with visitors who had crowded in to witness the unusual sight. Granny Wolf sat on the floor, a stout shapeless figure, all in black, moaning as she swayed back and forth, just as her son had described, her mouth wide open, her eyes rolling in her head.

The first thing to do was to have her removed from the confusion and dirt of that small house to the clean surroundings of the hospital. Her son brought her, and then waited with her while Elizabeth gave her a mere whiff of chloroform to relax the muscles, and reduced a double dislocation of the jaw.

The old woman revived immediately, and began to fumble with trembling fingers at the waist-string of her full gathered skirt for her "fire-bag". Her son took it from her, filled the pipe with tobacco, and lit it. Her whole attention was fixed on him, without the least regard for Elizabeth's questioning, beyond a disinterested "I was just yawning". Then, with the pipe at last in her eager hands, she drew a deep inhalation of its smoke and sighed with content. "Hai. Hai. Now I can smoke again."

It would be her Indian patients whom Elizabeth would recall most clearly, though by 1909 her practice was extending into developing settlements between the Reserve and the river. Few of the latter cases made any deep impression on her memory, perhaps because they were not particularly unusual in general practice. The Indians she had come to know well; the settlers were recent and more casual acquaintances.

Two of the Indians, Alex Stick and Alexis Crossarms, she would recall for

137

their ability to endure pain without complaint, in the revered tradition of warriors. When Alex broke his leg, he came to her hospital from Island Lake, travelling all those difficult miles slung in a travois behind a single horse. He stayed at the Mission for six weeks.

Alexis Crossarms refused to stay. He had been riding across country when his horse stumbled in a badger hole and threw him. He was quite alone, and he set the broken leg himself. Then he strapped the injured leg to the sound one, and dragging both pulled and shuffled his way for more than a mile to the trail where he was found and brought to the hospital. There was no need to re-set the bone, and he refused chloroform while Elizabeth put the leg in splints. He insisted on returning to his own tent to wait out the required six weeks before the splints could be removed and he might walk again. A few years later, he slipped on an icy doorstep and fractured his hip. Elizabeth set it, but his age prevented proper healing; and again he chose to stay in his own house, living for another two or three years, in pain and bed-ridden, but stoic to the last.

There were accidents with guns, of course. One cost light-hearted Johnny Heathen his forearm. He had been making a round of his trapline, and at one point stopped to kick the snow aside, his hand resting on the muzzle of his gun. His foot struck the trigger. Gangrene developed in the torn hand, and the arm had to be amputated above the elbow. Yet Johnny became so expert with his one arm and the stump that remained, it seemed to hinder him very little.

For David Quinney, the accident with his gun was fatal. He had been married for only a few days, and his young wife went duck-hunting with him in a boat they had covered with brush for camouflage. When David reached quickly for his gun, the trigger caught, and the whole charge of shot penetrated his abdomen. The terrified girl brought him to shore and ran for his brother's help. David was brought to the hospital. Elizabeth wired to Lloydminster for another doctor. She agreed to be anaesthetist, but the operation left her sickened by the other's rough and callous work. There was little or no hope for David in any case, and he died of general peritonitis.

Guns were involved in two other cases, both in white settlements, one manslaughter, the second deliberate murder. In the first case an English homesteader, a boy of eighteen, rode from Fort Pitt to notify the doctor and surrender to the Police. He had shot and killed his neighbour, a man old enough to be his father, a long-time resident in the west, who had used every means to intimidate and drive out the young settler. In one instance, he had lassoed the boy and dragged him across the country behind his horse. Then he had driven his cattle over the boy's crop, and riding down upon him had defied him to shoot. The boy shot and killed the man, but was acquitted as having killed in self-defence.

The second case had more than the usual element of horror since the murderer was a supposedly helpless paralytic, a Swedish homesteader in the bush to the north-west, whose mad jealousy of his wife drove him to kill her brother. While they were finishing the chores one night, he had dragged himself to his gun, and hidden it beside him in his bed. He shot the brother as he entered the house, and would have killed his wife too, had he been able. She escaped for help, but in a state of shock that left her bewildered for weeks. Elizabeth brought her to the Mission, where she might have stayed indefinitely on staff, had not the urge to prove her claim to the homestead drawn her back to clear the land. Her husband died of a second cerebral haemorrhage while awaiting trial.

These were cases that Elizabeth could not forget. There were many others that white settlers would remember with gratitude, cases that were routine work to a general practitioner, with obstetrics playing a considerable part. In many of the homes, she witnessed the hardship, the loneliness, often the desperation of women particularly, under conditions that she came to associate with the word "pioneering"; and so, in later years, she would say with earnest conviction, "But I was never a pioneer. My husband was John Matheson, and his experience and ability shaped my life."

Twenty-Nine

Her practice, her family, the Mission school—these were the three components of Elizabeth's life, woven together, taking their form and meaning one from the other, but having as their central force the compelling inspiration of John Grace.

Her practice required frequent travelling. For difficult trails or a distance that meant camping and the tending of horses, she always had a driver. On the Reserve, or to settlers' homes within a range of ten to twelve miles, she drove Malin; and the doctor and her beautiful pacing mare became known throughout the country.

The band of horses numbered more than thirty, including a standard-bred stallion and mares; and most of them were kept at the ranch near Fort Pitt, which was in full operation, with a herd of one hundred cattle, and for a few years sheep as well. Napoleon Parenteau, who was Charlie's older brother, was the foreman at the ranch, and Tom Rivard, a Montana cowboy, was in charge of the outdoor work at the Mission.

When settlement required enforcement of the herd law, the ranch had to be fenced. One night, a thunderstorm stampeded the horses, and four of the standard-bred fillies entangled themselves in barbed wire, lacerating their chests, and severing the tendons of their front legs. As soon as he found them, Nap came to the Mission. John Matheson was away, and Elizabeth took Gladys with her to the ranch.

The colts drooped in the shelter of a clump of poplars, unable to move any farther. Elizabeth examined them and went skilfully about her work, tying the severed tendons with strong kangaroo gut, snipping the lacerated flesh, inserting drains of rolled gauze, stitching the torn skin. Nap backed the wagon to where the colts stood quivering with pain and fear, and made an incline of planks from the end of the wagon to the ground. Then while Elizabeth and Gladys carefully moved the front legs of each colt forward in turn, he pushed and lifted their hindquarters, until all four were crowded into the wagon box, and could be hauled slowly and safely to the Mission.

The stable was practically empty during the weeks of summer. A few driving horses grazed in the pasture with the milk cows; the work horses were at a camp some miles from the Reserve, on land leased for haying. Tom Rivard was in charge of the work there, with a few of the older boys, and men hired for the season. Any chores at the Mission had to be left to the girls.

Nap stayed to place the colts in separate stalls, with strong canvas slings to support them; and then Gladys took charge, with Riema and Manias as her assistants. If the stable was to be a hospital it had to be specially clean; and the three of them went to work in the stalls with buckets and brushes, and then scrubbed the log floor on their knees.

A night or two later, a party of surveyors arrived, the Mission a supply base for their camp in the northern bush. They drove their horses into the stable, then hurriedly backed them out, to pasture the tired animals instead, and tender their own apologies for the mistake they had certainly made. Not in any of their experiences had they found another stable like that one; nor, for that matter, stable help to whom it was so pleasing to apologize.

Homesteaders, Mounted Police, Hudson's Bay Company clerks, all might have told them that. Gay chocolate boxes were blossoming at the Mission, bright with Gibson girls and ribbons; Tom Rivard was singing to Manias of flowers she had never seen, in the "land where the blue grass grows"—

When you wore a tulip,
A big yellow tulip,

School-house at Anglican Mission. Classroom on first floor,
staff rooms and boys' dormitories above.

St. Barnabas Church, built after 1883. Rebuilt on stronger
foundation (1904-1905) by John Matheson.

Mission House in 1913, enlarged year by year from original
four-room dwelling of 1892.

And I wore a big red rose.
'Twas then you caressed me,
And Heaven blessed me,
What a blessing
No one knows. . . .

And little Kathleen, with her quick ear for a tune, was learning others just as strange:

O the moon shines tonight on pretty Redwing. . . .

On the steamer Alabama
He was there at that pianah. . . .

Gee whiz! I'm glad I'm free.
No wedding bells for me.

While the life of the Mission went forward with all the eagerness and laughter of youth.

It was good to have the girls at home, but Elizabeth was concerned for their future, and pleaded still for further training. Not that year, their father insisted. They were happy; and they were certainly helpful, particularly to their mother, while their lively spirits animated the whole tone of the Mission. It delighted their father's heart that they were quick and willing workers, for it was the Mission that still came first in John Grace's mind.

He had been able to establish a small day-school as an out-post at Frog Lake, with Charles Quinney as teacher. Charlie had been one of the boys in the Mission school that first winter, and John Grace had sent him then to Emmanuel College in Prince Albert to train as teacher and catechist. From there, he had gone to mission work at Cumberland House; and now the Bishop had agreed that Quinney should teach the new school at Frog Lake, John Matheson having undertaken to pay the annual salary of two hundred dollars himself.

Emmanuel College meanwhile had been re-established as a divinity school under Archdeacon George Exton Lloyd as Principal. And in 1909 it was moved to Saskatoon to be affiliated with the new University of Saskatchewan.

One of its first graduates was a young Plains Cree, the Reverend Edward Ahenakew, who came to be John Matheson's assistant in 1912. He had been born in 1885 on the Sandy Lake Indian Reserve, where his grandfather's brother was Chief Ah-tah-ka-koop (Starblanket); and through his grandmothers he was closely related to Chief Mistawasis, Chief Poundmaker, and Chief Red Pheasant.

His own people were House Cree, who had hunted for the Hudson's Bay Company house at Fort Carlton; and John Matheson had known them since 1869. Ten years earlier than that, the first Ahenakew's brother, Napāskis, and John Grace's uncle, Donald Matheson, had accompanied the Earl of Southesk during his travels in the territory of the Saskatchewan. "A bold intelligent young man," Southesk had noted of Napāskis; and of Donald Matheson, "a jolly handsome Scotsman, singing snatches of gay songs all the day . . . tall, straight and merry—the image of a gallant young troubadour. . . . Cheerful in prosperity, gallant in adversity."

From 1877 to 1879, Edward Matheson had been the teacher at Mistawasis and Ahtahkakoop Reserves, years before Edward Ahenakew was born, and had always held a warm regard for his namesake, and pride in his achievements as a scholar and athlete at Wycliffe College in Toronto and at Emmanuel.

So, in 1912, Edward Ahenakew did not come as a total stranger to the Mathesons at Onion Lake; but it was at the Mission that the true cornerstone was laid of a friendship that would remain constant all his life. From the start, the girls drew him into their lively companionship; but it was to Elizabeth Matheson that his ability and his loyalty were to mean most during the five difficult years ahead. "You always knew where you stood with her," he would say. "Her friendship was never lightly given, and to have won it is something that I prize."

There were other members of staff who would have the same high regard for Elizabeth, and whom she remembered with gratitude and affection. Some stayed for years, but many who gave good service stayed for only a year, some for briefer periods.

Teachers were most difficult to find, and truly qualified ones impossible. One succeeded another, and though a few were quite unsatisfactory, most were able enough instructors for the elementary requirements of reading, writing and simple arithmetic, the usual level then in rural schools.

That the Indian children should learn English was the first requisite, and that was part of all the day's activities, though the insistence was not too rigid when many of the staff members spoke Cree readily and Indians who knew no other language were daily visitors at the Mission.

By 1912, several white children were day-pupils at the school, families of Sergeant Hall, Laurence Lovell, and Lang Turner. The latter had come in

143

1905 as clerk to the Indian Agency, and his children were all girls, constant playmates of the two youngest Mathesons who, for that reason chiefly, never learned to speak Cree as their older sisters had. Their brother's associates, with the exception of the Lovell boys, were Indians, and he learned to speak Cree with an easy fluency that was encouraged by Edward Ahenakew, to compete with them in games, and to prize the bow and arrows that Big Bear's son, Peter Thunder, made for him.

He was only nine years old, and it would be another year before he would enter St. John's College in Winnipeg. In the meantime, for him and his little sisters, life at the Mission was itself a varied and enriching education. Letitia and Grace found at St. Alban's a centre for their interests, and they came back to the Mission only for holidays. It was for Gladys and Riema that their mother felt most concern during 1912.

It was not easy to convince their father that they should be sent away for any training. What difference could that possibly make for girls? They would marry and never need to earn their own living.

That was an argument that had no weight for Elizabeth. It was not a question of marriage, she insisted, or of earning a living. She wanted her girls to have what she had, the independence and self-reliance that practical training could give. No, not Medical College; neither girl was inclined to such intensive study; they knew too well the sacrifice that course could require, and the effort. Nursing though did appeal to both of them. To that John Grace could agree. If Gladys would teach the school for a year, then she could take her training in any good hospital she chose; and Riema could go later.

Considering all the time and care that Gladys had given to those injured colts, however, he decided there should be some immediate reward. They could walk again, even trot a little with an awkward, stumbling gait; and they would have value as good brood mares. "Choose one of the colts," he said to the girl. "Whichever you want."

She asked Nap for advice. Which colt should it be? He grinned, scratched his head. Had Mr. Matheson said that? Just "one of the colts"? Well, Kate's colt hadn't a scratch or blemish on all her lovely gleaming body. Choose that one.

And John Grace, surprised, asked in his turn, "One of the colts? Just that? Well, a bargain's a bargain." And he nipped her glowing cheek, his own eyes twinkling. "What can one expect of an old horse-trader's daughter?"

Then Anson Lewis, the young homesteader who had named the community of Harlan for his home-town in Iowa, recalled the training he had begun in law. "Make that binding," he advised her, "with a bill of sale." And he drew it up for her. Now what had she given to make the transaction legal? "Just love and affection," she decided, and wrote those words in before she brought the paper to her father to sign. He read it with due care. "N'tanis, I give you back love and affection. That makes the agreement void." She had one dollar. She gave him that, and changed the bill of sale to read, "in receipt of one dollar."

Two years later, she sold the young mare and a new colt to the Reverend George F. Trench, the highly regarded clergyman who supervised student ministers in the Lloydminster belt of missions among white settlers south of the river. He paid her two hundred dollars. A fair return, Gladys thought, for one dollar.

Neither she nor any other of John Grace's children ever tried to estimate the measure of love and affection, and its returns.

Thirty

Elizabeth had another fine driving mare to succeed Malin. There were no papers for Minnie B. but she was said to be of the Dan Patch strain; and she had been a racer until her owner's unscrupulous training had barred her from the track.

John Grace had found her in Battleford, drawing a milk-cart, her owner reasoning that since he could not race her, she had to serve some useful purpose. Matheson made a fair offer, and Minnie was released from her drudging penance. She was a gentle beautiful driver for the doctor, and her speed was soon noted.

Bob Beattie, who ranched across the river, came to the Mission one day, driving a team of broncos. "Fastest little broncos in the whole country. Might beat old Dan Patch himself. Want to race them against that mare of yours? I'm ready to bet. . . ." John Grace had stopped him. "None of that. I'm not a betting man. Too wise for that now. And too old to race."

He turned to Elizabeth. "Willing to take Beattie on?" Her eyes were lively. But they couldn't race on the Mission trail. McCleneghan would have the news all over the country before the race was won. There was a level stretch a mile west, and if Elizabeth didn't drive ahead, Beattie would have his race all the way there and back, for she'd never be able to hold the mare.

As they neared the far end of the level stretch, Beattie drew up beside her. "This where we start?" Elizabeth nodded her head, all her attention given to the excited mare. On the instant, Beattie wheeled his team, and yelled at them. The race had begun, and in that same startled moment, Elizabeth's control of the mare was lost. Minnie B. whirled at the wild yell, the buggy rocking, inner wheels grating as they scraped the side. Then she shot ahead, cutting in so closely that the broncos had to veer from the flashing wheels, giving her a clear lead that she steadily increased as she lengthened into full racing stride.

Later Beattie remarked to Matheson, "You can preach against betting, but how about a sermon on the commandment that begins, 'Thou shalt not covet thy neighbour's wife?' " In the minutes of that race, Elizabeth had been young again, all swaying grace and laughter above careening wheels, hazel-green eyes flashing in the excitement that kindled her face to glowing colour.

But there should have been limits, she held, to the confidence others might have in her skill as a driver, and to the demands that John Grace's own pride could make upon her.

There was the day she would never forget, when Robert Chief came for her to say that Ka-nē-pa-tā-tāo was sick and needed the doctor. Charles Draycott offered to harness her horses. He had been a Mounted Policeman for more than twenty years before he retired to a homestead, and had driven four-in-hand for the Commissioner at Battleford. At the Mission stable, he hitched the stallion and a spirited gelding to the democrat.

They were waiting at the door when Elizabeth came from her dispensary, a beautifully matched team. There had been resistance to that hitching though, and they were still trembling. She could see the marks of Draycott's whip along their flanks. Without a word to Draycott, she turned back to find John Grace, and she was trembling too.

"He's harnessed Tom and Klondike for me to drive," she cried. "You'll have to tell him you'll not allow it."

"*I'll* have to tell him. Why can't you? Your pride? Well, there's mine too. If this is a trick of Draycott's, we'll be the laughing-stock of the country. He's no fool when it comes to horses. He knows you can handle them. Just keep their heads apart, that's all. Now get out there and drive."

His hands shook, his face was drawn and tired, his voice was that of an impatient old man. Elizabeth left the room. Anger with both men darkened her eyes as she stepped to the driver's seat and took the lines from Draycott. Robert Chief sat on the floor at the very back of the democrat. At least he could jump if there was trouble.

Elizabeth barely nodded to Draycott, but as the democrat moved past him, he raised his hand as though he would have saluted and lifted his hat to

146

her instead, repeating the warning, "Keep their heads apart, Mrs. Matheson."

The gate was wide open, and the horses swung to the road. She did not slacken the lines, and the powerful horses kept their swift pace along six miles of trail. As they came to the sloping hill that led to Ka-nē-pa-tā-tāo's house, Elizabeth's clear voice called a peremptory command to the men lounging near the door. Two of them jumped to hold the horses as she slowed them, gripping each bridle.

She attended her case, a routine one whose details would merge into all the other cases that she would have no reason to remember. One fact was to the forefront of her mind. She would have to drive those horses home alone. Then Robert, eyeing the sharp slope to the level road, said, "I'll come that far with you."

She held the horses to an unwilling walk down the hill, traces swinging low as the free-rolling wheels pushed the tongue of the democrat forward against the yoke. Suddenly, with a sharp clank of its chain, one trace slipped from its hook and dropped to the ground at Klondike's side. He started, and then stopped in obedience to her voice and her hand on the lines, just as the stallion had. Robert had jumped at once. He picked up the trace, fastening it quickly, one wary eye on Klondike's heels. Then he pulled a short length of shagginappi from his pocket, and tied that about the hook. "It'll stay now." He smiled in reassurance.

The quiet behaviour of the horses had restored Elizabeth's confidence, and she smiled in return. "I can manage now." The horses moved forward and broke into a quick trot at once. Looking back briefly, she nodded almost gaily to the Indian as he stood watching.

The horses quickened their pace, wheels humming on the sandy trail. The lines seemed alive in Elizabeth's firm hands, and she had to check her own excitement, a mounting delight in the speed and power of her team.

A group of big boys were at the Mission gate, and she knew who had set them there to wait. They ran to unhitch the horses swiftly and lead them to their stalls. Elizabeth walked across the Mission yard, and faces smiled from almost every window. John Grace waited in the doorway of "the Indian room". It was when he moved to meet her that she realized again, and with swift compassion, how old he looked. The last of the anger that had been a tight clamp about her heart was gone as suddenly as it had come.

"So you're home again. That was quick time. I knew you'd have no trouble."

A picture (one of the last) taken of John Matheson as he watched the school-children play at their picnic on May 24, 1913. Notice the moccasins which he always preferred to wear.

He was sixty-four, she had to remind herself, not seventy-five, as the doctor in Rochester had stated. That had been the year before, when she had persuaded John Grace that he must have a surgeon examine the small sore on his lower lip, that she was certain was "smoker's cancer".

He had agreed to go quite readily. There was business he could see to in Winnipeg anyway, and the doctor there would know, and operate if necessary. It was not until he was leaving the Mission that she had sensed how disturbed he was. She was haunted by that all day, and the next morning she left hurriedly for Lloydminster herself, telegraphing him from there that she was on the way. It was his sister Eliza who met her train at Winnipeg. John Grace had decided that he would go to the Mayo Clinic in Rochester for a thorough examination, and had left before her telegram arrived.

Elizabeth followed by the next train. She had sent no word, but when she walked into his room at the hospital, he said, "I knew you'd come, Bessie." The operation was in plenty of time, and left his lip thin but not noticeably scarred. There was no recurrence of malignancy.

She used the opportunity in Rochester to register for clinics, and at one was dismayed to find that the subject was her own husband. The surgeon's opening remark was a further shock. "This is a man of seventy-five." She heard herself exclaiming, "Oh, no, sir. Not seventy-five. Only sixty-three."

In the hushed room, the surgeon's angry glance fell upon her. "What, may I ask, do you know of this case?" "He is my husband." The surgeon waved his hand sharply. "Clinic dismissed, gentlemen." Elizabeth walked in humiliated silence to the door. As a doctor, she had been in error, and it was she who had been dismissed. The clinic could be resumed in another room, where no wife would interrupt the surgeon's discussion of the case, a man aged far beyond his actual years.

And yet, when John Grace returned to the Mission, he seemed his usual active self, and Elizabeth put the incident from her mind.

When spring came in 1912, he prepared once more for the trip to Edmonton, travelling by the Canadian Northern Railway from Lloydminster, but building his scows as usual on the river bank at Edmonton, to bring his goods down the Saskatchewan at high water.

Other traders, some of them newcomers to the Lloydminster area, followed the same practice, though not always with John Matheson's success, lacking his experience and his trained men. On one occasion in these later years, he had himself almost lost his life.

He had never carried insurance on himself or on his goods. It would have been difficult or even impossible to secure in the earlier years; and the very idea of insurance was contrary to the whole philosophy of his work, implying to him a lack of faith in God to whose service he had committed his life, his strength, his ability.

To make certain that such confidence should not become self-pride, he had hung a large illuminated text on the wall of his room: "Not by might, nor by power, but by my spirit, saith the Lord." And he lived by that, yet still withholding none of the might nor the power.

On the trip that had ended so nearly in tragedy, the weather was uncertain, and the scows had to be moored each night, side by side, one of them much shorter than the other. The men slept in their camp on the river bank, but John Grace rested only briefly, remaining in constant vigilance. When the wind increased and a thunderstorm broke, he went down in the darkness to the scows, testing the security of the goods, strengthening the lashings of the ropes.

Standing at the end of the longer scow in the blackness of the night, he jumped to where he thought the other one lay, forgetting the difference in length, falling into the deep channel of the river. As he fell he had thrown himself sideways to grasp the edge of the shorter scow with the tips of his fingers. Only his head was above water, and the strong sweep of the current pulled his body beneath the rough timbers of the scow. He shouted, but the crashing of the storm was too loud, and he had to wait for a momentary lull to shout desperately again before he heard an answering shout and the thud of running feet.

Tommy Slater had been disturbed and wakeful too, aware that Matheson had gone down to the scows. He was the youngest of the men, but the one upon whom John Grace most relied, and he came swiftly, guided only by the shout, until a flash of lightning revealed that white head against the blackness of the river.

He would have reached for the straining hands but for Matheson's laboured warning. "Let them be. Pull at my shoulders." He pulled with all his young strength, but John Grace weighed two hundred pounds, and had to exert every muscle of his own strong body, as inch by inch they pulled together to drag him from the relentless current.

That year only men travelled with John Grace; but there were times when he accepted passengers, as he had with Miss Cross and Helen Marsh in 1902. Bishop and Mrs. Newnham and Archdeacon Lloyd travelled with him in 1906; and Mrs. Sibbald came another year, when she was returning from a holiday in Edmonton. Elizabeth would always regret that in 1898 she had had her only opportunity, and that had been denied.

Usually the scows carried only those hired for the work, though sometimes John Grace brought men who needed his help. "A friend of mine," he would say then, "an old friend." Major Stiff was such a one. When they had first known one another in Edmonton, he had been a prominent citizen, one of the original share-holders in the railway; but that was long past. Only the distinction of the title remained, recalling his early military training and the rank that he had held in the Edmonton Home Guard during the Rebellion. At the Mission, that rank was used with unfailing courtesy.

John Grace had met him staggering along a street in Edmonton. "Why, it's the Major!" he said cheerfully, and Stiff mumbled, "Who're you?" Matheson could not resist the quip, "General Boulanger, looking for my white horse." The old soldier straightened at once, and his blurred vision distinguished the familiar face. "You're Matheson," he muttered, "Jack Matheson." He would have stumbled on, but John Grace gripped his elbow. "Where're you going?" "To beat the devil out of a man." The answer was prompt. "Then I'm going with you. That's my job now —beating the devil out of men." And John Grace led him to his poor lodging.

When the scows were ready, he found the Major again. "You're coming with me down the river. Do you good," he insisted. And for two years, Major Stiff was at the Mission, teaching music in the school, and helping in much of the general work.

He was shingling a roof the morning that the wagons assembled for the long trail to Edmonton, those two years later. Suddenly he flung his hammer aside, hurried down the ladder to snatch his few belongings, and swung himself onto the last wagon as it pulled from the yard. He died that winter in a fight.

For William Buchanan there was a better outcome. He was an illiterate Irishman, but he had been a soldier too, first against the Fenian raids that threatened Upper Canada, and then as one of Colonel Wolseley's men on the arduous trek along the Dawson Trail to the Red River in 1870.

He was a giant of a man in an army that had traversed six hundred miles of wilderness, building roads, making forty-seven portages, hauling heavy boats, packing guns, ammunition and provisions. Each cumbersome barrel of salt pork, each awkward arms chest weighed two hundred pounds, and some of the men would carry two of these over portages, boastful of their strength.

Buchanan had been a man well into his thirties, and John Grace twelve years younger when they first met in a saloon in the roistering village that was Winnipeg. Someone had set up a wager. Let the Irishman show his strength—the power of this frame so muscular that he boasted that his ribs were solid sheets of bone. Here was Jack Matheson, all two hundred pounds of him, seated in a strong chair. Lift him, chair and all. Buchanan knelt behind the chair, slipped his arms through to grasp the front rungs firmly, and then slowly stood, holding chair and man at arm's length, before lowering him with the same easy strength.

It was an experience that John Grace did not forget. But in Edmonton, all those years later, Buchanan had become a human derelict, a tall gaunt man with a straggling white beard, and thin hair that the wind lifted and tossed in long strands about his bald pate.

Rescued from the squalor of his life in Edmonton, he came down the river with John Grace, to live at the Mission for years, with periodic disappearances to his homestead in the bush, returning haggard and more silent than usual to his anchorage at the Mission. John Matheson had restored self-respect to him, and Buchanan repaid the debt with loyalty and a remarkable strength that continued into great age. He hoed potatoes, he mended fences, he cut and split endless piles of wood for insatiable stoves—and when Matheson's strength failed, the aged giant lent his own in patient, devoted attendance.

Thirty-One

In June of 1912, at Edmonton, the river was rising with the rush of water from the melting snow of the mountains; and the weather was hot. It bothered John Grace. This was the worst thing about growing old, he grumbled. Down at the river, the young men worked steadily, seeming to enjoy the heat, while he hurried about the hot dusty town, driving himself to complete the business of trading, buying and loading the scows.

It was on the street that he collapsed suddenly. When he regained consciousness, he was in hospital; and he stayed two days, fretting constantly. Tommy Slater was directing the building of the scows, but he was young and inexperienced, and it would be hard for him to keep the others at it. And then there was the loading to supervise.

Rest? How could they expect a man to rest with all that on his mind, and the bedsprings creaking and swaying with every move he made? Enough to make him sicker than any touch of the sun could. Give a man a straw palliasse and wooden slats to his bed—or the good firm earth beneath, and stars above, and the river rushing past.

And with that, he was up and out of the hospital, and back to the scows; and they were loaded and ready for the sweeping rush down the Saskatchewan. He brought them to a safe landing in three days of wondrous weather. It had only been the sun, he told Elizabeth, nothing more than that; but the doctors never told a patient anything, and he had not waited for any report.

She accepted his word at the time. The weather had been hot, and the explanation plausible enough. Then in mid-July, he collapsed again, and though he made the same quick recovery, Elizabeth knew that each time it had been a cerebral haemorrhage, not sun-stroke. He tired easily now, and he moved without his former vigour, like an old man.

Summer holidays ended, and the routine of the school year began at the Mission once more. Riema and Manias were the cooks; Gladys their mother's assistant and teacher as well. "She has had no training as a teacher," the Inspector, W. J. Chisholm reported, "but her natural aptitude for her duties is exceptionally good; she has picked up some of the best methods with beginners, and she infuses considerable energy into the work of all classes."

It promised to be a happy year for the girls, community activities stirred in the young settlements, and they had many friends. Mrs. Sibbald, with no daughters of her own, was delighted to be chaperon to Elizabeth's, and was often a hostess too, for she loved to entertain.

Her home at the Agency lent itself to this, whether in summer with its garden and croquet lawn, or in winter when the dark spruce trees were shrouded in snow, and birch logs in the fire-place of her drawing-room threw their bright gleam on fine period furniture, flowered cretonne, and shining silver.

It was her "drawing-room", just as the small body of water between the Agency and Mission—which anywhere else in that area would have been called a "slough"—was "Sibbald's pond"; and Mrs. Sibbald planned a skating party for the young people, as soon as the ice was firm enough.

It was the end of October then, and Elizabeth had to go to Edmonton to attend to some business that had arisen unexpectedly. John Grace had always seen to those matters, and this was the first time that he had asked her to go instead; but none of the business was strange to her, for they were equal partners in all transactions; and when he asked her if she would go in his place, she agreed as though it had always been their practice. The trip would not be the long and difficult one of earlier years, though it would have to be a rapid one, for the river crossing at that season could be awkward. She would have to leave at once, before the ferry at Hewitt's landing was out.

The reason that John Grace gave for staying at the Mission was simply the pressure of other work; and he was in good spirits again, enjoying the liveliness that the girls imparted, pleased to have them with him. They, on their part, were looking forward to the evening of skating on Sibbald's pond, as well as to a dance early in November, at a settler's new house, when two Hudson's Bay Company clerks would be their escorts, and Mrs. Sibbald the chaperon.

They hoped that there would be snow by then, so that they could travel smoothly in a sleigh to the accompaniment of bells, and that the ice would be firm enough soon for Mrs. Sibbald's skating-party. They would wear their red pleated skirts, white jumbo-knit sweaters with high turtle necks, and their red toques and mittens. Would mother please look for gaily woven L'Assumption sashes in Edmonton to wear with the sweaters?

Elizabeth reminded them that she might not be able to return before then; that ice on the river could delay her. And freezing temperatures did come, and snow. High up the river, ice formed and broke away, drifting down the open channel. Ferries had to be taken out. And business delayed their mother in Edmonton.

Winter had begun, but the weather was fair, the snow easily cleared from Sibbald's rink for the party. John Grace walked over to the bonfire to watch the young people skate. The next evening, however, when the girls appeared at the supper table in their prettiest dresses, he was surprised; he had quite forgotten that the dance at Roberton's house was to be that night.

Two parties, two late nights, one after the other. "Remember," he told them, "you may dance all night, but you'll still work all day." And they reminded him that there had been no slackening that day for either of them. Their young charm beguiled him. "Be home early," he said when they were leaving, and then stood listening until the sound of sleigh bells and their laughing voices was lost in the distance.

In wintertime, work had to begin and end by lamplight, and usually by nine at night the Mission was silent, the lights all out. It was then that John Grace made his careful inspection, to be certain that no lamp was left burning, and that every fire was out or safely banked with ashes.

It was not quite nine when he began his rounds that night. He needed to carry no lamp, for the moon, shining on white snow, reflected its light into all the familiar shadowed rooms. Only the hallway was dark, and he was moving through it when his dull ears detected the voices of Tom Rivard and Manias. They were to be married in March, when she would be nineteen, and this was the one hour that they had to themselves, when all the work of the day was finished, and the Mission was silent.

John Grace turned sharply at the unexpected sound. Directly in his way in the dark, there was a post, one of several in the Mission house supporting ceilings where partitions had been changed and rooms enlarged or altered. High up in this one where a lamp could be hung a large nail had been driven. The head struck and penetrated his right eye.

In the shock of that moment, he jerked himself free, and staggered back towards his own room, stopping at the foot of the stairs to call to his young assistant, "Ahenakew, come . . . I'm hurt," before he fell unconscious. Tom and Manias heard the sudden cry, and ran with Edward Ahenakew to carry John Grace to his room. There was haemorrhaging, but they knew only one remedy for injury to an eye, and they applied raw beefsteak. Then Tom ran to the Agency for help, and Mr. Sibbald came, though all that he could do was sit beside the unconscious man until his daughters should return.

There was no way to let the girls know, except by messenger, and that would bring them home no sooner. Yet Gladys would always say, "I knew that something had happened. I knew at nine o'clock." She could not admit that she was tired, but her spirit was suddenly quenched. Riema was drifting by dreamily in a waltz, but Gladys ran to Mrs. Sibbald. "It's a quarter to twelve," she said breathlessly, "and we promised Papa that we'd be home early." Mrs. Sibbald laughed. "Nonsense, my dear. Nine o'clock, that's all. Even twelve would be too early to leave."

And so it was past two o'clock when they neared the Mission and Gladys could see the lamplight in her father's room. She knew then that something indeed was wrong, even before Rivard ran out to open the gate for the sleigh; and she cried out, "How long has my father been dead?" "Not dead," he answered, "but unconscious since nine o'clock."

As they ran into his room, John Grace roused. "It's you, Bessie," and then when Gladys spoke: "N'tanis, I'm glad you've come, but I had hoped it was your mother."

Riema helped her at first, and then Gladys stayed to apply boracic compresses continuously to his eye, from early that Friday morning until late Saturday night, still wearing her party dress, crushed and stained.

"Keep the news from your mother until she's home," he begged. "Tell McCleneghan that or those keys of his will be clicking it out."

Elizabeth did not arrive in Lloydminster until early Sunday morning. Because of the river, she was advised to start at once for Onion Lake, and she hired a team at the livery barn. The driver could help Hewitt break a passage for the boat, and she telegraphed the Mission for a team to meet her on that side.

It was late afternoon when she came to the river. On the far shore, Edward Ahenakew waited with a sleigh; he had been there for more than an hour Hewitt told her.

The main channel was still open, but the men had to clear a way for the boat through thickening ice on both banks, and the crossing was slow. The wind was cold and darkness was falling. That and the long delay seemed reason enough, Elizabeth thought, for Ahenakew's silence as they drove. He gave only brief answers to her questions, which was unlike him, but still an Indian's way, and she accepted it, as she did the speed to which he urged the horses. It was a distance of only nine miles, and she was eager to be home.

At the Mission, gusts of wind whipped the snow across an empty yard. Lamps were lit in the house, and as the sleigh drew up, the door of "the Indian room" was flung open, and Gladys and Riema ran to meet her. The tremor in their voices alarmed her, though she could not see the marks of tears on their faces.

"Where is your father?" "At his desk," they said, and then in a burst of feeling, "We're so thankful you're home." But Elizabeth was hurrying to John Grace's room. He was sitting at his desk, his back to the door, his head bent over some papers. When she spoke, he moved the swivel chair slowly

155

around, and she saw the bandage that his white hair had concealed.

At her cry, he said casually, "Just an accident. Struck my eye on a nail in one of those posts." And then with deep thankfulness, "Everything will be all right now you're home, Bessie." She removed the bandage and lifted a lamp to look closely at the eye. He spoke querulously then, "How can you see anything with that piece of striped calico over the light?"

Her hand trembled as she set the lamp down, its clear flame mocking her through the polished glass of the chimney. She would not withhold the truth. "There's no calico. Your eye is badly hurt. Why didn't you send for a doctor? Why wasn't I told that this had happened?" But all he said was, "I'll have to lie down. Help me to my bed."

The girls ran to help him, Gladys crying, "He wouldn't let us tell you. I've done my best. When you were coming, he made us help him to his desk so that you wouldn't be alarmed."

She was sobbing, and John Grace took her hand in his, repeating, "Now your mother's home, everything will be all right. I know it." But not the sight in that eye ever again, Elizabeth knew. Yet it was weeks before she could persuade him to go to Edmonton for treatment; and when he did go, he stayed for only a few days in hospital. "They weren't doing anything for me," he insisted, "that you haven't done better here." By February she had convinced him of the danger to his good eye, and he agreed to go to Winnipeg to Dr. Harvey Smith, who operated, removing the damaged one.

Nine years before, Dr. Smith had been a lecturer at Medical College, and Elizabeth knew his skill. She remembered a clinic when he had described a serious eye condition and had asked, "What would you do for this case, Mrs. Matheson?" And she had laughed, "What would I do, Dr. Smith? I'd send the patient straight to you."

Thirty-Two

John Grace had run his last scows down the Saskatchewan. Times had changed, he agreed, and supplies for the Mission could be freighted from Lloydminster. As for trade in furs, he could never resist the finest when they came his way, but there were buyers all through the country now.

Cattle were more profitable, and the ranch had proved a sound investment. It was a competitive venture certainly, and there were some who thought that the old missionary should keep to his proper work, and leave ranching to them. That he was successful only strengthened prejudice. It ap-

A family portrait, 1913. Dr. Thomas Scott, with his son (*at left*) and daughter (seated between Selkirk and Ruth Matheson at front) visited the Mission when he returned from Ceylon in 1913. John Matheson (*at right*) had suffered two strokes and the accident to his eye, and objected to being photographed. His resistance affected the others, particularly Elizabeth and Gladys. Elizabeth's mother, Mrs. James Scott, is on Elizabeth's right. Kathleen is on her father's knee. *Standing at back, from left to right*: Letitia, Gladys, Riema, and Grace.

peared that the only sure way of forcing him out would be to discredit him, and one rancher did not hesitate to try.

He charged Matheson with having sold cattle that were not his own. And he had evidence to prove it: hides bearing the accuser's brand, from steers sold under Matheson's name. The date of the sale and the total number sold tallied with those that Matheson had himself selected to be driven from the ranch for shipment to the buyer.

There had been one miscalculation however. Nap was called to the Mission to explain, and when he realized the full significance of the charge against his old benefactor, he confessed that he had been bribed to permit the substitution of three steers bearing the other rancher's brand, when the cattle selected for sale had crossed the river. The charge was promptly dropped.

The incident shocked Elizabeth. "I thought that man was a friend." "Not in this business," John Grace reminded her. "But I called his bluff." "And what'll you do about Nap?" "Why, nothing. He should have had more sense, but the bribe was tempting. I should have made sure myself this couldn't happen. Anyway, Katie and Vester Brown need a place to live.

157

Might as well be the ranch. He and Nap can keep an eye on one another. There'll be no trick like that again.''

But Elizabeth knew there could be others. There had been others that had failed, and some that he had simply brushed aside and forgotten. The shared responsibility was hers, but never the zest that John Grace had for involved business deals and speculative trading.

And now, when he was no longer alert as he had been, there was this increased anxiety on her part that some error in judgment might ruin them and their work. She had to be constantly watchful, knowing that newcomers were convinced that his business ventures had built up a private fortune, and that his generosity only indicated how easily he might be persuaded to part with some of it.

A visitor one day noticed that a patch of psoriasis on Matheson's shin was annoying him. ''I'd give a hundred dollars to anyone who could cure this for me,'' he said irritably. Elizabeth had told him there was nothing that would give more than temporary relief. His visitor had another opinion. Back in his home county, there had been an old woman who could cure anything, and he had some of her ointment with him, a secret preparation.

He brought it to the Mission the next day. John Grace tried it, and the irritation eased. Elizabeth tested the ointment and recognized a popular patent medicine. ''Zam-buk. Samples of that in every mail. A lot of use it'll be. He needn't have bothered to put it in another tin either.'' But she had not heard John Grace's statement, and he had forgotten about it.

When the man called again, there seemed no reason to deny him the satisfaction of a kindly act, nor to tell him that the doctor was certain the psoriasis would return. And the settler reminded him then, ''You have a note of mine for two hundred dollars. Here's one hundred in cash to pay it. You said you'd give a hundred to anyone who could cure that.'' Contemptuously, Matheson gave him his note. It had been a smart trick.

Others might be honest enough, but still expect too much. Elizabeth learned to inquire about the reason for any visit to John Grace's room, and if necessary to make the excuse to appear there herself.

One day she had surprised John Grace at his desk, pen in hand, preparing to sign a paper. The homesteader standing beside him was embarrassed at her appearance, her husband vexed by her question. It was a minor matter, he said, nothing that she needed to worry about, just a note he was backing for a man who needed his help.

For how much? Uneasily then, John Grace named the sum. Two thousand dollars. Elizabeth's anger flared, and she gave the unsigned note back to the settler and asked him to leave. She had humiliated both men, and any relief that John Grace might have felt at her timely interruption vanished. "It's no use," he said to the other man. "You can see what I'm up against."

The words stung, but Elizabeth was compelled to accept the role. The problems of the school were becoming a burden to him now, and though she sought his advice, its administration fell more and more upon her shoulders. In addition, her practice was growing as settlements developed; and there was above all her concern for her husband and their family.

Gladys had completed her year as teacher, and would begin her training in the Winnipeg General Hospital in January of 1914; Riema assisted her mother; Letitia was withdrawn from St. Alban's for a year, to teach instead.

"I was a bit difficult," she would recall. "Truthfully, I can say that I was defiant; and that may have had something to do with the decision to keep me busy at home for that entire school year. It was good for me. I can remember going to the empty sitting-room in the early winter evenings, and staying there alone to think things through and plan my next step.

"One of the pupils, William McKay, was not a year younger than I, and he treated me with disdain. He had come to school too late to adjust, and he would speak Cree in my hearing on every possible occasion, thinking that I couldn't understand him. Once, when I had given some order, he replied, 'Nomoya katache, moonias squasis' and that meant, 'I will not, you little white girl.' I was big enough to take the strap to him in my exasperation; but it wasn't long before I realized that in William I had the same problem that the mistresses at St. Alban's found in dealing with me.

"I faced that in those sessions alone in the dark sitting-room, and I came out of it a different person. Even William recognized that, and reacted helpfully. I had to work it out on my own, taking no one into my confidence.

"When I returned to St. Alban's in September, I had changed my attitude. I remember the new housekeeper stopping me one day during the first term, to ask if I was Leita Matheson, and to tell me, 'I was dreading your return to school because of what I had heard of you from others, but you are not the girl I expected.' I knew what she meant. The rest of my school days were a revelation to me; and though the awakening was late, it lasted. William McKay may have taught me more than I taught him."

W. J. Chisholm, when he made his report as Inspector of Indian Agencies and Schools, was much more complimentary to the girl. "The teacher, Miss Leita Matheson, is but eighteen years of age and had had no special training for her work. She has, however, fair scholarship and is unusually well adapted to the work of the school-room. She is alert and energetic, and has easy and complete control of her classes. A lively interest is created and well sustained. Her education was received in part at St. Alban's College in Prince Albert, where well qualified teachers are always employed; and her methods, if largely suggested from her own experiences as a student, are rather well adapted and successfully employed."

"Successfully employed." To encourage her pupils in English, she stressed reading. "Sing the words," she would say, to lift the children from the dull monotone of mere words. "Sing them like this." And she would raise her own lovely voice in singing words. Or read aloud herself.

One afternoon she chose to read *The Wide Wide World* to children who knew no world beyond the Mission and the Reserve; and at one particularly heart-rending passage, when the wicked stepmother had hurled the child's kitten into a tub of scalding water, she closed the book firmly and laid it on the desk. "There. Anyone who wants to know what happened, can read the book for himself." And one small entranced girl took her first bold step into the wondrous wide wide world of books; and little Kathleen was left to mourn, "Ruthie never plays games with us now, or sings hymns. All she wants to do is read books."

Thirty-Three

The teacher who succeeded Letitia at the Mission school was a cousin several years older than the Matheson girls, John Grace's niece Anne Cunningham. She had been a member of staff for brief periods in the earlier years as a girl, and then had taught at Lac la Ronge. She returned to the Mission a mature woman, with the authority and competence of experience; and to her ability she added a loyalty and an affection for Elizabeth that went back to childhood when she had been a little girl at Poplar Point and Elizabeth had been her teacher.

With Anne Cunningham in the school and Edward Ahenakew in the work of the Church, these essential departments of the Mission were strengthened; while a third new member of staff came to serve with equal efficiency in her own important domain of the kitchen.

Mary Ann Robinson was short and stout and no longer young. All her early training had been in the household of a Dowager Duchess of Northumberland, far removed from the Indian Mission where she gave devoted service. She had come to Canada in 1912 to be with friends; and it was the good fortune of the Mathesons that she had accepted employment, first at the Battleford School, and then at the Mission.

160

The Battleford Industrial School was closed in July of 1914, as part of a changing policy in Indian education. Day schools were expected to serve Reserves in that area; and the newly built Mackay School at The Pas would take children from more remote areas where hunting and trapping prevented any settled life.

For years, John Matheson had pleaded for some enforcement of the regulations relating to the education of Indian children, stating in a letter to Ottawa in 1906, "The Indians know well that we are unable to compel them to send their children to school and they take very good care to show us that we cannot do so. . . . On this Reserve there are at least eighty children of school age."

In 1914, there were still only seventeen Treaty Indians on the school register at the Mission; and to Ottawa these children constituted the enrollment, and the only justification for a school that was located on an Indian Reserve, however many other children might be enrolled as boarders or day-pupils.

The Department of Indian Affairs considered closing the boarding-school and having an "improved day-school" in its place; and Bishop Newnham and Archdeacon Mackay both endorsed this. John Matheson offered to board and clothe the children who came from Frog Lake and Island Lake. But Mr. Sibbald, the Agent, reminded the Department that many of the Indians still hunted and were away for long periods from the Reserve, with their families. He considered it unlikely that a day-school would be successful.

As for the boarding-school, Indians who had shown little interest before now begged that it should be maintained, and there were several prospective pupils from Frog Lake, and Island Lake, and from Thunderchild's Reserve too. For years it had been difficult to reach the Department's quota of twenty in the Mission school; now they were requested to raise the number to thirty and then to forty, with accommodation assured.

The Bishop wrote to Ottawa concerning John Matheson's possible resignation for reasons of health: "Considering his age and the faithful work that he has done for many years, I do not feel that I could ask him to resign. I have had the school and the mission visited and inspected lately, with the result that I would ask for further consideration or delay in closing it. Mr. Matheson is in very bad health and cannot possibly continue to hold the position very long. Meanwhile it would break his heart and probably kill him to close the school. I would ask that the closing be dropped for the present."

The Department concurred. "Rev. Mr. Matheson has devoted the best portion of his life to Indian work and is deserving of consideration. Although

161

he is not by any means as energetic in his management as he once was, fair work is being done, and it is doubtful whether another competent man to replace him could be found. In view of these conditions, the boarding-school may be continued, as they have a competent staff, and the school is economically managed.''

Bishop Pinkham had not tried to find any answer to his own puzzled ''How so much can be done with so little visible means is simply wonderful.'' But now, in John Matheson's failing health, when the burden of financing was too heavy for him, Bishop Newnham had to face that problem. He turned for advice to practical men of business.

Of course, the Mission's financial statements were nonsense. No auditor could possibly accept them. Per capita expenditures of about $70—and all those children well-fed, decently clothed and housed? Salaries for the principal and for his wife as teacher or as medical officer—listed as receipts but rarely as expenditure? And finally those items:

1901	-	$1,458.25	from private sources;
1902	-	$1,966.33	from other sources;
1903	-	$2,589.20	private funds;
1904	-	$2,445.33	from private funds;
1909	-	$ 750.00	from private funds;

Whose private funds? Why, if a man gave of himself, his family, his substance like that, he would have to be a saint; and no one had ever called John Matheson *that*.

Then what about the Mission itself? ''The land on which the buildings are situated and that used in connection with the school belong to the Reserve. No surrender was ever made, and consequently no transfer to the Church, which has only the usual right of occupancy.'' This from the Department, which refused to consider the purchase or rent of the buildings.

Buildings? Certainly, the Diocese had built the original four-roomed house, and the sagging church that had had to be rebuilt on a new foundation. Who had paid for that? Who had authorized and paid for all the other buildings?

The perplexed Bishop wrote to the Department, ''You doubtless know that Rev. J. R. Matheson has always been hard to handle, and that it was impossible to get full and accurate financial statements. But at any rate he did the work, kept the school going and out of debt; and claims that it was partly with his own money. In the same way, he and his wife claim that they found nearly all the money for the various buildings.''

162

A few months later, he wrote with more certainty: "The Church as a Corporation could do and did comparatively little for these buildings and stock. Various church members may have contributed at times, but the Rev. J. R. Matheson was responsible for the revenue and expenditures. He never once called on the Indian Department to pay his deficit or overdraft, but put his own personal income and earnings into the school property for the time being. Neither the Church nor the Indian Department had the right to expect him to do this. We owe a debt to him and his family."

Thirty-Four

The outbreak of the Great War had its effects at Onion Lake. Young men went from the settlements, and Indians enlisted, though they were not subject to compulsory service. The awful battles were followed in press reports; the misery of trench warfare translated into feverish knitting of socks and Balaclava helmets; the anxiety and pain of casualty lists experienced every day.

Herbert McCleneghan had introduced a rural telephone line in 1913, and now he read the war news from the telegraph station as it flashed over the wires to Edmonton. One long ring would sound on every telephone to call listeners. At the Mission, the cry would be taken up at once: "War news, Mrs. Matheson, war news"; and she would hurry to the telephone, her slate and pencil ready, to write her own bulletin of the news in swift clear notes, hours before boys on the streets of Edmonton and Winnipeg would be crying, "Extra! Extra!"

From month to month Elizabeth's responsibility grew as John Grace's health failed. He was no longer able to leave his room, and William Buchanan's strength lifted him from bed to chair. Rosalie's cheerful daughter, Carrie, assisted in caring for him, and his two little girls were with him daily for the noon meal.

They were the only two at home that year. Riema had joined Gladys in training at the Winnipeg General Hospital; Selkirk was at St. John's; Letitia and Grace at St. Alban's.

Their mother's letters went out to each one. It was a practice that had begun when she had first left them to complete her own studies, that resumed when they in turn went away to school, and would continue without faltering throughout her lifetime.

The schools made weekly letters the rule, and hers in return conformed to this pattern in regularity, but they were individual letters, written for each particular reader, and with the stamp of her personality in some quick turn of phrase, some wry and witty comment.

Over the years—with no intent beyond her own love—they wove into a strong entity a family that would always be scattered, that might count in brief years, even in months, the actual time they could remember being all together.

In January of 1916, Riema suffered a serious attack of rheumatic fever that left her heart damaged. Her training at the Winnipeg General Hospital ended, and not until April was she well enough to travel back to the Mission. Gladys brought her home, but returned to complete her final year of training, and was not free to be with the family during the summer holidays.

For each one, the years at the Mission would hold a special place in memory. They were years that had drawn their vitality and meaning from John Grace, and that faltered with his closing life.

One simple thing could still please him. He had always loved the stirring evangelical hymns—hymns that told of grace and forgiveness, of over-shadowing and upbeating wings, of beauteous isles and rivers, of refuge from the storms of life. He would have his children sing these to him while he listened, joining when he could in certain lines and verses: "The sands of time are sinking"—it was not that he had lived to great age, but that within his shorter and most active life he had experienced much, compassed much, lived intensely. Even now, he:

> Wrestled on towards Heaven
> 'Gainst storm and wind and tide—

never before had he asked to lean upon one stronger, until now:

> Lord, grant Thy weary traveller
> To lean on Thee as guide.

For this last, most difficult of all trails was long and wearisome; his heart old and tired.

"Dark, dark has been the midnight"—the midnight of pain and suffering, of helpless aching body, of weary dragging limbs, of slowly clouding mind—to one who had been strong, and swift, and keen.

"But daylight is at hand"—still that eager expectant face, turned not

164

towards a distant settlement, waiting as long ago for the sunrise, but now to see:

> The glory dawning
> In Emmanuel's land.

John Matheson died on August 25, 1916. In a letter to Gladys, Elizabeth wrote, "You must not worry about me, my tannie. I am well and trying to bear my load, although I do not seem to see how I am to get along without your father. He had not been able to help me lately, but he was here, and now I am so alone, and no one behind me if I fail."

She did not fail. At the beginning of 1916, Bishop Newnham had written to Ottawa, "This carrying on of the work by women alone, without a responsible head, is not satisfactory." Now, at his request, Elizabeth consented to carry on for another year, while he looked for a successor.

"The school," he wrote, "will henceforth be managed in a more orthodox manner according to Indian Department rules and regulations. Previously, in view of the fact that Mr. Matheson was finding the finances and that no one else could have run the school without greater aid from the Indian Department and the Church, he was allowed a pretty free hand by us."

The enrollment of Treaty Indians doubled; and the Department, "recognizing the untiring devotion of your late husband and yourself to the moral, physical and intellectual development of the Indian children committed to your charge," concurred in Elizabeth's appointment as principal.

"I do feel," the Bishop wrote again, "that it is up to the Indian Department to stand by us and take a share of the load." Finally this was achieved, the government assuming the cost, not only of operation under another principal, but of building a large Indian Residential School about seven miles from the previous site.

The old Mission House was torn down then. To newcomers it had seemed at best a strange and rambling assortment of rooms; and it was the kindest service they could render, to leave no desolate haunted walls.

Elizabeth faced troubled days. Her three youngest children were in school; Letitia and Grace not yet qualified teachers. Riema's health would continue to be a matter for concern, but her heart made its own fair compensation, and her spirit supplied the rest. Though she would not outlive her mother, she would make hers too an active, satisfying life, disproving at

165

Elizabeth with Gladys and Selkirk in Winnipeg (1917) before Gladys went overseas with the Canadian Army Medical Corps.

least in part the advice of doctors who said that she should not marry nor have children. Of all Elizabeth's family, only Gladys was earning her own living in 1917, and she had enlisted as a nursing sister to serve with the Canadian Army Medical Corps in England and in France.

Their mother's income was small, for the maintenance of the school had been John Grace's primary concern to the end. He had continued to oppose the idea of insurance—even the clergy pension scheme—as a negation of faith. Edward Matheson was not of that opinion, and had been diocesan secretary for the pension plan from its inception. So firmly did he support its policy in fact, that he paid the fees for some of the older clergy who had felt as John Grace did, or who simply could not find the money.

He and Elizabeth had long since agreed that John Grace's fees must be paid, with or without his consent. That gave her a pension from the clergy widows' and orphans' fund of one hundred dollars at first, and then of four hundred a year. Even the hundred dollars helped. She had been able to sell the cattle and horses; and over the years would realize some small returns from the land that John Grace had acquired.

She applied to the Department of Indian Affairs for re-appointment as government doctor, asking that her salary be raised from its level of three hundred dollars during all those years, to one thousand. She would provide her own transportation and residence.

The lower floor of the hospital building had been converted for that purpose. She hoped that the Department would buy the log building for a hospital, but when this was refused she arranged to have it taken down and rebuilt on land to which she had clear title, in the hills just outside the Reserve, to the north-west of the Mission.

The question of the salary troubled her. Had she asked too much? She knew that there were men in the area who would welcome the security, and would take the work from her if they could, on the excuse that she no longer had the strength for arduous trips. She was fifty-two, and she herself thought that she could have few more active years, and was concerned for her children.

When her appointment at one thousand dollars was finally confirmed, she had already accepted a position in Winnipeg at the same salary, but for half-days only; and she could keep her children with her there. Dr. Mary Crawford was superintendent of medical inspection in the public schools of that city, and the work was being extended. She had known Elizabeth at the Ontario Medical College for Women, and late in 1917 she advised her to apply for the position of assistant medical supervisor. Elizabeth did so at once, and was accepted, her work to begin in March of 1918.

Before she left Onion Lake, she made another trip into the northern bush. An old Indian was dying. There was no help that she could give him except the reassurance of a doctor's presence. It was a long trip, but he had been John Grace's friend.

The weather had been mild for some days, and her driver grumbled about the soft condition of the roads. Elizabeth paid little attention, her own thoughts turning to other trips that she had made over these same trails in the years that were now ended. Lonely for that past, uncertain for the future, she was moved by the sense of another presence. It was with her for long moments, so real that she said his name aloud, "John—John Grace." The team stopped. "Something wrong?" her driver asked.

She was brought sharply back to an awareness of her surroundings. Ahead of them was the expanse of the lake, crossed by the winter road. She said, "We'll not go this way. Turn the horses. We'll take the summer trail."

"Every track goes this way," he objected. "We'll have to break the summer trail, and it'll take us an hour to drive around the lake. We'll be across in ten minutes this way. The house is just over that rise." "Turn the horses," she repeated.

Sullenly he turned them; but she felt alone again, conscious only of the difficulty of that trail as the horses broke through crusted drifts of snow. They moved slowly. As they approached the house, a son of the family met them. "How is the old man?" Elizabeth asked. "He died about an hour ago." He looked along the trail that they had broken. "It's good you came that way," he said. "No one's crossed the lake today. The ice seemed to give when we crossed yesterday."

In Winnipeg, Elizabeth bought a house. It had to be large, but it was without pretention—a home to be lived in, whose furnishings told the story of a family—the piano from the Mission sitting-room, John Grace's desk of bird's-eye maple, his swivel chair, the brasses from bazaars in India, the brightly beaded saddle and gauntlets of a Plains Cree, the casual possessions of children, a student's books, a boy's school cap, the scarlet and blue of a nursing-sister's military cape—all the dear disarray of home—the first family home that Elizabeth and her children had ever known together.

It seemed to ring with buoyant happy life. It knew the continuing joy of hospitality, the sound of dancing feet, the laughter and song that were an echo of John Grace's own zestful spirit.

There, apart from school hours, Elizabeth could devote herself to her family. With John Grace had gone the high enthusiasm, the compelling inspiration; and yet the years that followed for her were happy, in the sense that they were serene, the vibrant tones muted, the passion spent.

Postscript

Half-day employment in the schools was extended to full days; the few years that Elizabeth had expected to work seemed to extend indefinitely. The question of her age became a matter of some embarrassment to her. She spoke of resigning—there was no question of retirement on pension; she had been over-age when she was appointed, and on half-day employment at first, to preclude such a possibility. The Board asked her to continue until Dr. Crawford retired, though there was a difference of ten years in age.

168

Portrait of Elizabeth Matheson, 1934.

In June 1941, Mary Crawford retired, and Elizabeth Matheson's resignation was accepted. She was then seventy-five years old.

For another fourteen years, she was able to travel freely usually by air, spending her winters in Texas with Gladys, her summers in Canada with all the others of her family.

Elizabeth Matheson died in 1958 at the age of ninety-two, her spirit bright to the end. Her body was returned to the Mission churchyard to lie beside that of John Grace, fulfilling a promise given more than forty years earlier.

She had died in San Antonio, Texas, in Gladys's home, two thousand miles from the Saskatchewan; yet the long journey proved to be right, bringing her back to the people and the place where she belonged. "I'll feel that I've come home," she had said.

On the day of the service in July a rodeo was in progress on the Reserve, a mile or two from the church; among the crowd attending the rodeo, few could have known Elizabeth Matheson, though they remembered the name, and observed three minutes of silence.

The church itself could not hold all who came, and many listened from outside to the opening hymn:

> Now thank we all our God,
> With heart and hands and voices . . .
> Who from our mother's arms
> Hath led us on our way
> With countless gifts of love. . . .

The Archdeacon of the Diocese conducted the quiet service of Evensong, with its *Nunc Dimittis*: "Lord now lettest thou thy servant depart in peace. . . ."

Canon Edward Ahenakew was the preacher, speaking in English and then in Cree for the Indians who made up half the congregation. People had come from Prince Albert and Lac la Ronge, from Battleford and Edmonton, from Balcarres and Saskatoon.

Rosalie's daughters joined the family in Lloydminster, Carrie travelling from Calgary. Their brother came from Cold Lake.

Riema had died in 1955, but Elizabeth's five remaining daughters came from Texas, Sault St. Marie, Winnipeg and Regina to join her son in Lloydminster. There the long cortege assembled to travel north to Jumbo Hill and the ferry-crossing of the Saskatchewan, and along the familiar way to the site of the old Mission.

170

When the graveside service of committal had ended, there were the gentle greetings of old friends in English and soft Cree. Two women stood by the twisted maples of Elizabeth's garden, the older one Jimmie Crookedneck's daughter, a pupil in the early school, her English long unused.

"She wants to say," her companion explained, "that this is where she had to be today. Your mother was the best friend she ever had." At the graveside, two men waited to return the earth. They were Robert Chief's grandson and Johnny Heathen's son, named James Scott by Elizabeth's mother.

Another man watched in silence. He was Ben Quinney, more than ninety years of age, erect still, and clear of mind, who remembered Elizabeth as she was in 1892 when the Mathesons came to St. Barnabas Mission, and who would recall her friendship with Mary, the wife of his young manhood.

In 1949, Elizabeth Matheson had attended the meetings of the British Medical Association in Saskatoon, and was interviewed for the Canadian Broadcasting Corporation. She was asked:

"When you look back over all those years, what do you think?"

"Think?" she repeated, in her clear vibrant voice. "I would go back and live them all over again—every one of them. But how I wish I had had the knowledge that we have now, and all the advances in Medicine. I could have done so much more."

After her retirement, when she had leisure enough and her active interest in life continued still, Elizabeth Matheson kept a journal. Entries often referred to the years at the Mission, recalled by the date or a person mentioned. Towards the close, she used a card for marker, and on it she had written these lines from Shakespeare:

Fear no more the heat o' the sun,
   Nor the furious winter's rages;
Thou thy worldly task hast done,
   Home art gone, and ta'en thy wages.

Bibliography

KILDONAN SETTLEMENT

Hargrave, J.J. *Red River*. John Lovell, Montreal, 1871.

Matheson, Archbishop S.P. *Reminiscences*. Winnipeg *Free Press*, 1933-39.

Pritchett, J.P. *Red River Valley, a Regional Study, 1811-1849*. Ryerson Press, Toronto, 1942.

Ross, Alexander. *The Red River Settlement, Its Rise, Progress, and Present State*. First published 1856. New edition—Hurtig Publishers, Edmonton, 1972.

TERRITORY OF THE SASKATCHEWAN

Butler, William Francis. *The Great Lone Land*. First published 1872. 17th edition, Burns and Oates, London, 1910.

Griesbach, Maj.-Gen. W.A. *I Remember*. Ryerson Press, 1946.

Hughes, Katherine. *Father Lacombe, The Black-Robe Voyageur*. Moffat, Yard and Co., New York, 1911. McClelland and Stewart, Toronto, 1920.

MacKay, Douglas. *The Honourable Company*. McClelland and Stewart, Toronto. Revised edition, 1966.

Macoun, John, M.A. Canadian explorer and naturalist. Assistant Director and Naturalist to the Geological Survey of Canada, 1831-1920. *Autobiography of John Macoun, M.A.* A Memorial Volume published by the Ottawa Field Naturalist Club, 1922.

Southesk, The Earl of. *Saskatchewan and the Rocky Mountains*. First published in 1875. New edition—Hurtig Publishers, Edmonton, 1969.

Stanley, George F. *Birth of Western Canada*. University of Toronto Press, Toronto, 1960.

Steele, Col. S.B. *Forty Years in Canada*. McClelland and Stewart, Toronto, 1917.

Published articles:

Laut, Agnes. "1500 miles down the Saskatchewan". *Toronto Saturday Night*, Christmas issue, 1908. *Scribner's Magazine*, April 1909.

Lyle, G. R. "Eye Witness to Courage" (Barr Colonists). *Saskatchewan History*. Vol. XX, No. 3, Autumn 1967.

Murray, Jean E. "Early History of Emmanuel College". *Saskatchewan History,* Vol. IX, No. 3, Autumn 1956.

Unpublished articles:
Clinkskill, James. "Recollections". Typescript, courtesy of Mrs. Paul Prince, now in possession of Gardiner Church Museum, Battleford.
McKay, the Hon. Mr. Justice James. Papers of the McKay family, courtesy of J. Fortescue McKay.

Periodicals:
The Guide. Bound copies of the Battleford Industrial School paper, 1895-1899. From the library of Canon E.K. Matheson. Microfilm, Saskatchewan Archives.
Lloydminster Times. Microfilm, Saskatchewan Archives.
Saskatchewan Herald. Files. Saskatchewan Archives.

Public Documents:
North-West Rebellion Trials 1885. Queen vs. Scott. Saskatchewan Archives.
Sessional Papers 1896. Report of the Inspector of Indian Schools. Saskatchewan Archives.

ST. BARNABAS MISSION AT ONION LAKE

Mission Reports, Diocese of Saskatchewan. Oxford Press, Toronto, 1900-1909.
General Correspondence, Department of Indian Affairs, 1893-1918. Public Archives of Canada.
Letters concerning the Protestant boarding-school at Onion Lake. RGIO — 72/596, File 658-1, Vol. I.
Letters concerning the Mission hospital, 1917-1918. RGIO. Vol. 4081, Black Series, File 481279.
Reports on the Inspection of the Church of England boarding-school, 1912-1916. RGIO Vol. 6323, File 658-6.

WOMEN IN MEDICINE

Manitoba Medical College Library records. Courtesy of the Librarian in 1939, Miss Ruth Monk.

Neatby, Hilda. "The Medical Profession in the North-West Territories", *Saskatchewan History*, Vol. II, No. 2, May 1949.

Shortt, Mrs. Adam (Elizabeth Smith, M.D.C.M.). "The Women's Medical College", *Queen's Review*, Kingston, 1929.

Stowe Gullen, Augusta, M.D. "A Brief History of the Ontario Medical College for Women". Printed in 1906.